Advance Praise for *Called to Serve*

"In *Called to Serve: The Inspiring, Untold Stories of America's First Responders*, readers will get to know some of America's finest. Emergency medical technicians and paramedics reveal behind-the-scenes accounts of saving lives and saving themselves as they are dispatched in their ambulances. Police officers, a sheriff, and constable share their heartfelt stories of not only solving crimes and arresting bad guys but highlighting what good police work is all about. Finally, firefighters, many of whom have had to deal with serious injuries as well as post-traumatic stress, give readers a window into their devotion to helping others and changing lives in the process. I know you will be moved and motivated by the stories in this extraordinary book by my very good friend Mike Hardwick and his co-authors Dava Guerin and Sam Royer."

—**JOHN RICH,** country music singer-songwriter, record producer, and activist

"*Called to Serve: The Inspiring, Untold Stories of America's First Responders* written by my good friend, Dava Guerin, and authors Mike Hardwick and Sam Royer, is a must-read for every American. In this important book, you will be moved by the deeply personal stories about first responders such as John (Woody) Woodall, as well as those who risk their lives for our health and safety and live by the oath they take to 'serve and protect.' When I was diagnosed with breast cancer, our family had to adjust. We were the recipients of a million acts of kindness. My daughters were in elementary school but that experience of seeing their mom bald and going through chemotherapy helped them connect to other families who had been diagnosed with cancer. Many of their friends over the years had parents affected by this awful disease. This experience helped our family build a degree of resilience that comes from learning early on that life can throw you curve balls and that none of us can get through those tough times without our friends, family, and neighbors who step in to help. A sense of gratitude will always be a part of our family's idea of service given how our lives were upended at that time. I think service needs to be something that you teach your children early. Service starts within the family. For us, we are grateful for the amazing first responders and veterans and cancer warriors whom we have met over the years. Their extraordinary strength has driven us to work hard every day."

—**JENNIFER GRIFFIN,** Fox News National Security correspondent

"Christians are admonished to give honor to whom honor is due. This includes the brave men and women who have dedicated themselves to protecting and serving the needs of people in perilous conditions. *Called to Serve* introduces us to a small number of heroes engaged in what is increasingly a thankless service fraught with risks for those who have chosen the path less traveled. We respect and honor our first responders for the high cost of their service to humanity. We thank the authors for blessing us with this book."

—**DR. CAROL M. SWAIN,** distinguished senior fellow for
Constitutional Studies, Texas Public Policy Foundation

"There are no better authors to bring us the stories of America's first responders in *Called to Serve* than Dava Guerin, Mike Hardwick, and Sam Royer, because they—like them—have public service in their DNA. What unites them with the everyday heroes we meet in the pages of this wonderful book, is a sense of optimism and positivity that can overcome even the biggest of obstacles. Especially in today's challenging times of wars abroad, a global pandemic, and hyper-partisanship at home, we need the kind of book that shows us that America still is a very special place, with communities throughout the country enriched by men and women living the dignity of public service on a daily basis. I hope every American will read this important and inspirational book."

—**PETE WEICHLEIN,** CEO, US Association
of Former Members of Congress.

"Fifteen stories from across the country recounting the bravery, self-sacrifice, and public service performed the unsung heroes among us—our first responders. These are people running toward danger when there is trouble. These are the people who seek no glory, who 'are just doing my job,' and who you hope you never meet but know you will when they are needed. These are real stories of real Americans just doing their job and I am so proud that we get to share their stories."

—**DAVID S. FERRIERO,** archivist of the United States

"While most flee the sound of danger, there are those who run to the roar. They are the best among us. With undeniable qualities not often seen since the time of our great-grandparents, first responders exist as living remnants of the Greatest Generation. Unasked are questions like how or why or when or where ... a simple YES is their only response when *Called to Serve.*"

—**ANDY ANDREWS,** *New York Times* bestselling author of *The Traveler's Gift* and *The Noticer,* founder of WisdomHarbour.com

"As someone who has spent a career in public service—from being a member of Congress, secretary of Agriculture and an advocate for many issues including eradicating hunger, restoring bipartisanship in Congress and others—I know the value of service. The dedication to making the world a better, healthier, and safer place for each and every American. When I had the pleasure of reading *Called to Serve: The Inspiring, Untold Stories of America's First Responders,* co-authored by my good friend, Dava Guerin, and her colleagues, Mike Hardwick and Sam Royer, I was moved by the heroes profiled in the book. From police officers who risk their lives during routine traffic stops or domestic disturbances, EMS professionals who are first on the scene during car accidents, and a myriad of 911 calls—to firefighters who have the emotionally taxing job of not only putting out fires, but trying to save lives in the process—*Called to Serve* showcases their tremendous heroism. Readers will take a journey with these inspiring first responders and will learn what motivated them to serve, and reveal behind-the-scenes stories of their lives in professions that inherently have danger at their core. They are America's unsung heroes. I highly recommend every American read this wonderful and enlightening book."

—**DAN GLICKMAN,** former cabinet secretary of agriculture

"What is it that makes some people want to dedicate their lives to serving others and making their communities better and safer places for all? And what keeps them on the job, day after day, year after year, despite enormous stress, great personal risks, and sometimes violence directed at themselves and others with whom they serve? The answers to these and so many other questions about those who put their lives on the line for the greater good can be found in *Called to Serve: The Inspiring, Untold Stories of America's First Responders.* Authors Mike Hardwick, Dava Guerin, and and Sam Royer take deep dives into the personal and professional lives of sixteen first responders—police officers, firefighters, EMTs. Readers will learn who inspired these heroes to serve, how they train for these grueling professions, and what kind of daily challenges they face as they encounter the very best of people—and sometimes the worst. This book is a reminder of how lucky we all are to have such self-sacrificing public servants in every corner of our nation. As the authors state, 'They make our world safer, healthier, and secure.'"

—**KEVIN FERRIS,** co-author of *Vets and Pets: Wounded Warriors and the Animals That Help Them Heal* and *Unbreakable Bonds: The Mighty Moms and Wounded Warriors of Walter Reed*

"*Called to Serve* is a wonderful peek inside the very heart and soul of our country's first responders. This wonderful book by Mike Hardwick, Dava Guerin, and Sam Royer should be required reading for every American who has or will need to call 911 one day. In other words, all of us. We need to learn more about the men and women who will show up at our door when we need help the most."

—**JEAN BECKER**, author and former chief of staff of President George H. W. Bush

"What authors Mike Hardwick, Dava Guerin, and Sam Royer have done by writing *Called to Serve: The Inspiring, Untold Stories of America's First Responders* is tremendous. It will not only be appreciated by those who have served, but most importantly, those who benefit from their service as well. The stories in the book are personal, touching, and uplifting. As a fire commissioner I know first-hand the sacrifices these brave Americans who risk their lives every day make and their dedication to service. *Called to Serve* will give readers an inside look into the life and work of these brave first responders. Thank you to the authors for writing this important book."

—**TOM MCQUEEN**, chaplain, fire commissioner, and author

CALLED
TO SERVE

CALLED
TO SERVE

The Inspiring, Untold Stories
of America's First Responders

MIKE HARDWICK, DAVA GUERIN, AND SAM ROYER
FOREWORDS BY JENNIFER GRIFFIN AND JOHN RICH

Skyhorse Publishing

The authors will donate 10 percent of the book's sales to the Gary Sinise Foundation to support its "First Responders Outreach" program.

Skyhorse Publishing books may be purchased in bulk at special discounts for sales promotion, corporate gifts, fund-raising, or educational purposes. Special editions can also be created to specifications. For details, contact the Special Sales Department, Skyhorse Publishing, 307 West 36th Street, 11th Floor, New York, NY 10018 or info@skyhorsepublishing.com.

Skyhorse® and Skyhorse Publishing® are registered trademarks of Skyhorse Publishing, Inc.®, a Delaware corporation.

Visit our website at www.skyhorsepublishing.com.

10 9 8 7 6 5 4 3 2 1

Library of Congress Cataloging-in-Publication Data is available on file.

Cover design by Kai Texel

Print ISBN: 978-1-5107-7181-9
Ebook ISBN: 978-1-5107-7182-6

Printed in the United States of America

This book is dedicated to our heroic police officers, firefighters, and emergency medical professionals who sacrifice their lives every day to assure our health and safety.

CONTENTS

PART THREE: AMERICA'S FIREFIGHTERS

FOREWORD

by Jennifer Griffin

Tikkun Olam: Repair the World

Called to Serve: The Inspiring, Untold Stories of America's First Responders written by my good friend, Dava Guerin, and coauthors Mike Hardwick and Sam Royer, is a must read for every American. In this important book, you will be moved by the deeply personal stories about first responders such as John (Woody) Woodall, as well those who risk their lives for our health and safety and live by the oath they take to "serve and protect."

When we lived in Jerusalem covering the Israeli-Palestinian conflict for seven years, my husband and I, both journalists who worked long hours while attempting to raise our two young daughters, were introduced to a Hebrew phrase that came to embody our approach to the next twenty years as a family: *Tikkun Olam*, "repair the world." It is an idea that comes from the belief that the world needs healing and that we as individuals can play a role in that quest to improve the broken world around us. When we arrived in Jerusalem in 1999 before our daughters were born at a hospital overlooking the Old City of Jerusalem, we thought we were going to spend the next years covering peacemaking. Instead, we covered conflict and reported on the human suffering that followed.

This came after years of war reporting in Africa, Afghanistan, and other parts of the Middle East. Our daughters entered the world after 9/11 and on the eve of the US military invasion of Iraq. When we returned to the United States and I began covering the Pentagon, the US wars in the Middle East were raging. Walter Reed hospital was filled with injured service members and their families as the surge into Iraq began and hundreds of thousands of US troops deployed to the Middle East.

A sense of helplessness turned into an opportunity to help those who had sacrificed so much following the terror attacks of 9/11. As a family we began attending the Walter Reed Christmas party at the invitation of some of the veterans groups who I had begun to know as a result of my work for Fox News and at the Pentagon. My daughters, who were in middle school at the time, would volunteer to pass out Christmas gifts to the wounded veterans and their families. They were the elves who delivered gift baskets and toys to the children of the wounded veterans. They became sensitized to the catastrophic injuries facing amputees and those with traumatic brain injuries in a way from which most American children were shielded.

This began a journey that changed all of our lives. My daughters Annalise and Amelia began volunteering at Walter Reed through high school at the video lending library where they would speak to and build friendships with wounded vets, many of whom were not much older than they were. This led to their advocacy for veterans seeking to bring their combat translators to the United States on Special Immigrant Visas (SIVs).

Five years later the entire country would be speaking of SIVs after the chaotic withdrawal of US troops from Afghanistan, but my daughters had been advocating for more SIV legislation and help for Afghan and Iraqi translators for years. They raised money for Track Chairs for double, triple, and quadruple amputees. That is how we all got to know a firefighter named John "Woody" Woodall, who volunteered to drive to New York from his home in North Carolina to help his NYC first responders after the 9/11 attacks. Woody became a close friend and he would entertain the wounded warriors and their families during the holiday parties at Walter Reed dressed as Elvis. Service was in Woody's DNA and he became a role model for my children, for whom service had become an important part of their lives.

When I was diagnosed with breast cancer, our family had to adjust. We were the recipients of a million acts of kindness. My daughters were in elementary school but that experience of seeing their mom bald and going through chemotherapy helped them connect to other families who had been diagnosed with cancer. Many of their friends over the years had parents affected by this awful disease. This experience helped our family build a degree of resilience that comes from learning early on that life can throw you curve balls and that none of us can get through those tough times without our friends, family, and neighbors who step in to help. A sense of gratitude will always be a part of our family's idea of service given how our lives were upended at that time.

I think service needs to be something that you teach your children early. Service starts within the family. For us, we are grateful for the amazing first responders and veterans and cancer warriors whom we have met over the years. Their extraordinary strength has driven us to work hard every day.

The idea of *Tikkun Olam* is at the core of how we behave as a family. Service has become a part of our DNA and there is no group who deserves our respect more than those you are about to meet in the following chapters, those working to "repair the world."

—**Jennifer Griffin**, FOX News National Security Correspondent

FOREWORD

by John Rich

I N THE AMERICAN SPIRIT, THERE LIVES A UNIQUE BOLDNESS OF CHARACTER and sense of duty when it comes to serving others. Among us, there are those chosen few who rise head and shoulders above the rest by dedicating their lives to doing the most dangerous, and often most thankless jobs, that carry with them the very real risk of life and death.

If America endured even one week without our police, firefighters, EMTs, paramedics, and volunteer first responders, we would devolve into total anarchy, resulting in the destruction of everything we hold dear.

Even in the face of culture that belittles, and even attacks, their lifelong dedication to serving others, these brave men and women still answer the call when trouble is at our doorstep. Their stories are legendary, but often unheard. They sacrifice their safety, and even their lives, on behalf of others. They leave behind a legacy of honor, tradition, and commitment that lives on to inspire future generations. They represent the best among us, and we salute them now and forever.

In *Called to Serve: The Inspiring, Untold Stories of America's First Responders* readers will get to know some of America's finest. Emergency Medical Technicians and paramedics reveal behind-the-scenes accounts of saving lives and saving themselves as they are dispatched in their ambulances. Police officers, a sheriff, and a constable share their heartfelt stories of not only solving crimes and arresting bad guys but highlighting what good police work is all about. Finally, firefighters, many of whom have had to deal with serious injuries as well as post-traumatic stress, give readers a window into their devotion to helping others and changing lives in the process.

I know you will be moved and motivated by the stories in this extraordinary book by my very good friend Mike Hardwick and his coauthors Dava Guerin and Sam Royer.

—**John Rich**, country music singer-songwriter, record producer, and activist

ACKNOWLEDGMENTS

FIRST, WE WOULD LIKE TO THANK THE HEROIC FIRST RESPONDERS IN THIS book for sharing their inspiring stories and risking their lives every day for our safety and well-being. Each has enthusiastically supported our project, and we thank them for their participation.

Jennifer Griffin, a hero in her own right, has written a thought-provoking and heartfelt foreword. For decades, she has volunteered her time supporting our wounded warriors and veterans at Walter Reed National Military Medical Center and beyond. Her love and support of our nation's warfighters knows no bounds.

John Rich is not only a masterful singer/songwriter, producer, and part of the country music duo Big & Rich, but he is also a philanthropist and activist. He has helped launch the careers of young artists, guiding them to reach success in their own right. His songs have inspired us, made us laugh, and helped us heal in times of strife. Most importantly, John Rich is the epitome of an artist who believes in paying it forward and encouraging Americans to support our nation's heroes.

To Gary Sinise, founder of the Gary Sinise Foundation, words cannot express our gratitude for your decades of service—from helping veterans, wounded warriors, and military members—to Gold Star families and first responders. You have given so much to improve their lives and motivated Americans to always do a little more to recognize and support their service.

To Amy Royer Vierling, we cannot thank you enough for your excellent editing and expertise in helping us to make the stories in the book come alive. Your insights and knowledge of the healthcare industry and first responders was invaluable. We could not have done this without you.

We also want to thank our friends and families for their wisdom, encouragement, and love, especially Ellene Fleishman, Kris Vierling, Jean Becker,

Nick Bivens, Megan Hardwick, Whitney Blessington, and Matt Clarke. Writing and researching a book is time consuming, and we appreciate their letting us spend time away from our families in order to bring these stories to life.

Our publisher, Skyhorse, has been a pleasure to work with over the past nine years. Their commitment to our nation's warfighters, veterans, and first responders is unparalleled. Our amazing Skyhorse editor, Caroline Russomanno, as well as Mark Gompertz have added their expertise and advice and we appreciate that beyond words.

Finally, to our first responders who have died in the line of duty: we salute you. Your service and sacrifice matter. We will never forget what you have done on our behalf. For your families left behind, know that you are in our hearts and prayers. And to the million-plus first responders in America, including law enforcement officers, firefighters, EMTs, and paramedics, we will always be there to support you and your unwavering dedication to service.

INTRODUCTION

It is part of the cop DNA: we are attracted to danger. Where others run from it, we—by nature and profession—run toward it.
　　　　　—Bill Bratton, former New York City police commissioner

THE FIGHT OR FLIGHT RESPONSE PRESENT IN ALL HUMAN BEINGS IS A physiological reaction to danger. For most of us, at the first sign of an attack or a threat to our survival, we would choose to flee and run away from the danger. But not for the unsung heroes profiled in *Called to Serve*; they are the ones who are running in.

We asked ourselves why any person would place themselves in harm's way and risk their health and safety to protect perfect strangers? Who are these people and why should we care?

We made the decision to write *Called to Serve* to answer this question as well as to highlight the inspiring stories of the intrepid first responders who have dedicated their lives to keeping us safe. By design, we chose not to explore the explosive issues regarding racism, defunding the police, or the aftermath of the George Floyd murder and the resulting worldwide protests. That is left for others to explore. Instead, we believe that 99 percent of law enforcement officers are decent and dedicated people; you will meet five of them in the first part of this book.

We were also fortunate to personally know many of the law enforcement officers profiled in the book, as well as the EMTs, paramedics, and firefighters. One other female firefighter we did not know but felt we had to include as she added to the book's depth and readability.

When the average American walks out the door to go to work, runs errands, or takes their children to school, they know their day will end as it began—back home. They often take for granted, at the conclusion of a xxii | Called to Serve

long day, that their families will embrace them with open arms—the cycle repeating itself day after day, year after year.

Yet, for the resolute men and women inspired to serve—including law enforcement, firefighters, emergency medical technicians, and paramedics—their future is less certain. As they put on their uniforms in the morning or are called to action in the dark of night, they place themselves in harm's way, often suffering from devastating physical injuries—even death—not to mention pernicious hidden wounds such as post-traumatic stress. Their families bear the burden as well, with spouses, parents, and children living with the reality that their loved ones may not be coming home, despite every intention of doing so.

According to the Officer Down Memorial Page website, as of July 2022 there were 136 deaths of officers killed in the line of duty, 633 who died in 2021 and, since the statistics were recorded, a total of 25,865. The majority of those deaths were caused by COVID-19; gunfire; vehicular assault, and others including automobile crashes, stabbings, and heart attacks.[1] The non-profit organization Blue H.E.L.P reported in a 2019 study that 228 American police officers died by suicide.[2] Suicide, tragically, is also an occupational hazard, including the four US Capitol Police and Washington, DC metropolitan police officers who died by suicide following the January 6, 2021 attack on the US Capitol. This is a national tragedy.

Our nation's firefighters, who risk their lives by saving our businesses and homes from the ravages of fire, also face serious on-the-job hazards. The US Fire Administration tracks their fatalities each year and found that, in 2021, forty-eight firefighters died in the line of duty.[3] Even more suffer from the physical injuries of firefighting including severe burns, smoke inhalation, explosions, and lung diseases, as well as invisible wounds such as post-traumatic stress and depression. Tragically, the suicide rate among firefighters has increased exponentially. For the past five years they have exceeded the rate of on-duty deaths by approximately 30 percent.[4] Among

---

1   "Annual Fallen Officer Statistics," 2022, Officer Down Memorial Page, https://www.odmp.org.

2   "2019 Study," Blue H.E.L.P, 2022, https://wwwbluehlp.org.

3   "Annual Report on Firefighter Fatalities in the United States," 2022, United States Fire Administration, https://usfa.fema.gov.

4   Ibid.

the most devastating calls firefighters experience are those where the death of children are involved or when victims die by suicide.

Emergency Medical Technicians and paramedics, which help more than twenty-two million patients in the United States every year, surprisingly, suffer the most work-related injuries, illnesses, and fatalities as their fellow first responders. The Bureau of Labor Statistics reports that on average, the injury rate for EMS professionals is three times the national average.[5] Their injuries can include overexertion, exposures to hazardous substances and infectious materials, falls, slips, and motor vehicle accidents, as well as trying to calm down patients with mental health challenges. But despite their own issues and work-related exposures, they remain dedicated to being there when we need them the most.

We hope you will be inspired by reading *Called to Serve* and understand what motivates and challenges these extraordinary Americans, as well as recognize their unwavering mission to serve and protect. From Sheriff Matt Crisafulli, who spent the majority of his career working with students to help them avoid drugs and alcohol, and Amy Royer, an EMT who saved countless lives, to Captain John (Woody) Woodall, who after 9/11, rushed to Ground Zero with his fellow firefighters to help locate and bury his fallen colleagues; he then created a 9/11 Memorial in their honor—each of these unsung heroes embodies the best of human nature.

There are many more of our nation's first responders with inspiring stories to tell. In a perfect world, we would have memorialized those whose service, character, and patriotism are exemplary; they deserve our admiration and respect. Perhaps in the future we will try.

We encourage you to support these dedicated first responders in your own community; they continue to serve and protect despite often insurmountable challenges. Keep them in your hearts as you go about your day. They deserve our gratitude, as well as acknowledgement that their service and sacrifice matter.

---

5   Bureau of Labor Statistics, U.S. Department of Labor, Occupational Outlook Handbook, EMTs and Paramedics, at https://www.bls.gov/ooh/healthcare/emts-and -paramedics.htm.

PART ONE

THE MEN AND WOMEN IN BLUE

One

Daytona Motor Officer with Heart

I am all that there is of the most real.

—Agatha Christie

ISSETTE DESCHAMPS IS A CLASSIC GEMINI. SHE HAS TWO DISTINCT PASsions that to some may appear incongruous. On the one hand, she is an indefatigable volunteer, raising money for a variety of nonprofit organizations including one she created to help the families of fallen police officers. She lives and breathes service and is there for her community twenty-four seven. Lissette is also a bad-ass motor cop—a five-foot-four beauty that has arrested her share of criminals, including murderers, child molesters, drug addicts, and prostitutes. She was among the first women motor officers in Daytona Beach, Florida. For the past twenty years, Lissette and her 2020 Harley Davidson Road King motorcycle have contained crowds, protected dignitaries, and rode into the hearts of the citizens of Daytona Beach, who counted on her to keep them safe. She has also solved major crimes in her positions in the Homicide Division as well as the Sex Crimes Unit of the Daytona Police Department.

Lissette was born in Midland, Michigan, though she only lived there for a few days in her young life. Her mother, who was very pregnant at the time, and Lissette's family were returning home from her grandmother's funeral when her mother began to experience excruciating labor pains.

They drove to the nearest hospital and just three hours later, Lissette was born.

Michigan, however, was just a temporary pit stop; Okeechobee, Florida was the Deschamps family's permanent home. Okeechobee is a rural, sub-tropical small town of five thousand people, according to the 2000 census. It also has the distinction of being the "Speckled Perch Capital of the World," the bucolic place where fishermen take advantage of Lake Okeechobee's abundant fish population. It is the perfect location for a young girl and self-proclaimed "tomboy" to grow up.

"Growing up in the country was great for me," said Lissette. "I was definitely a tom boy and used to wear my two brothers' hand me downs. I also loved playing softball and riding four wheelers and was obviously not like the other girls I knew in Okeechobee."

Lissette has two brothers—the oldest is Mark and the youngest Pierro. Mark is eight years older than Lissette and was always a troublemaker. For as long as she can remember, Mark was doing things that her siblings would never dream of—shoplifting, taking drugs, and breaking into cars, for example. As a result, he was locked up at a youth detention center. Lissette remembers visiting him at Thanksgiving and other major holidays during the time he was living there. Years later, Mark would commit the crime of all crimes, and would change Lissette's life in ways she could never have imagined.

While the family's base was Okeechobee, they traveled a great deal due to Lissette's father's job as a union welder. During the summers they would visit various states, including Massachusetts, Maine, and Tennessee. But by the time Lissette was about to enter high school she had had enough of moving from city to city. "I told my parents that I wanted to attend high school in one spot and not have to continue to travel," Lissette recalled. "It was tough having to meet new people and adjust to a new school. Thankfully, my parents agreed and let me stay in Okeechobee for the next four years."

But Lissette's mother had a problem with one of her newfound friends. "There was a neighbor in town who was my first female friend, and she was a few years older than me," Lissette explained. "I was shocked one day when she told me she was pregnant. When my mom found out, she would not allow me to hang around her anymore, so I had to focus on things other than my friends."

So, Lissette put all of her energy into sports. She played softball and soon became a varsity athlete. Yet there were few role models for a young woman who had little interest in getting married and having children. "In our small-town girls did not have much direction. In fact, people would joke that women from Okeechobee should be barefoot, pregnant, and in the kitchen. That was certainly not going to be me," said Lissette.

Lissette's parents divorced in 1989. And money was tight. But Lissette continued to excel in softball and did very well in academics. She met a coach, Russ Brown, who spent his high school years in Okeechobee and after graduating college moved back to help. He recognized her talent and suggested Lissette try out for a college softball team. "I was ecstatic that Coach Brown was behind me all the way," Lissette recalled. "He told me that my college tuition could be paid for if I were on the softball team, and since my mom could not afford to pay for college, I decided to take him up on the offer."

Lissette tried out for Brevard Community College's softball team and made the cut. She was offered a two-year college scholarship and was over the moon. She loved being part of a team and advancing her athletic skills. To finish her degree, she transferred to the University of Central Florida in Daytona. Lissette focused on her academics, majoring in criminal justice and minoring in psychology. During her two years there, she made the decision to become a social worker. Lissette wanted to understand why people like Mark, who grew up in the same family as she did, could turn out so differently. "I never could understand why we were all so different," Lissette said. "Why was Mark not like me, my mom, or my other brother? I decided to go into social work so I could help children with tough upbringings and give them some of the benefits my parents gave me," she added.

During her last two years of college in Daytona, Lissette experienced severe culture shock. "Where we grew up, we were never exposed to drugs or drug addicts other than the issues with Mark as he got older," Lissette said. "I remember when I was working at the Stuart Marchman Center, which is a resident juvenile adolescent twelve-step program, during college; I called my mom and told her how shocked I was. I said, 'Mom, you would not believe that there are thirteen-year-old girls here who are prostitutes and crack cocaine addicts.' She was not that surprised since Mark was using more and more drugs, always getting into trouble, and continuously being locked up."

At the Center, Lissette realized the harsh reality of many of these kids' lives and what they were lacking in terms of consistent parenting and support. "I felt like I had a good group of kids come in and do their time but, unfortunately, when they got out, there was no help for them on the street. Their parents did not support them. I realized that being a social worker would not be a long-term solution for the kids I was desperately trying to help. That is when I decided to make a significant career change," Lissette added.

In the back of Lissette's mind was always her troubled brother, Mark. "Perhaps if Mark had a police officer who could have set him straight, his life would have turned out differently?" she wondered. "Maybe I should become a police officer instead of a social worker, and that way I could have a front-line approach and help people before their problems even begin? Maybe if just one cop cared about my brother, he would not be locked up right now?"

Lissette was consumed by guilt and, at the same time, resolved to make a difference. She wanted to help her mother realize that Mark's issues were not the result of bad parenting. That he had a choice and made the wrong one. "We all have discretion," said Lissette. "I wanted to be the one kid that did it right and help my mom understand that my brother's issues were not her fault. I think that was the moment that I seriously realized I had to become a police officer."

While still working at Stewart Marchman, Lissette applied to Daytona State College's Police Academy. The course took six months to complete, and Lissette and one other woman were the only two in a class of primarily men.

Lissette was sponsored by the Daytona Police Department, meaning that they paid all of her tuition with the promise that she would fulfill a three-year contract as a police officer. Lissette was declined admission to the academy on her first try, because the officials said she did not meet the height/weight ratio. "At the time I thought that was ridiculous, because I was a varsity athlete and, at five foot four and 145 pounds, I was very strong and muscular and certainly capable of doing the job," she recalled.

For Lissette, the second time was the charm. She was admitted to the Police Academy and was excited to begin her new career challenge. "It was a tough course, for sure, and was challenging at times, but I always thought I was one of the boys anyway and could hold my own," said Lissette. "I grew up boyish and was used to hanging out with arrogant people, so being with a group of men never was intimidating." Lissette laughed when she recalled the day she was supposed to take the final exam before officially becoming a police officer. "The day of the exam I had to have emergency surgery on my wisdom teeth, and I had to re-take the test with my teeth packed. It was kind of funny to think about it twenty years later."

Lissette was twenty-four years old when she became a Daytona police officer. She knew right away where she wanted to be and what she wanted to do. "I always loved motorcycles and decided I wanted to be a motor officer. They were a different breed; top dogs; cream of the crop," Lissette said. "I told my sergeant that I wanted to ride a motor for Daytona. I could not believe it when he said, 'Lissette, that is not going to happen. You could not even pick up a bike, let alone ride one. You will have to choose another position.' I was beyond determined to prove him wrong."

Lissette was assigned to the night shift as a patrol officer while she continued to work on her dream of becoming a motor officer. She put in her application for a motorcycle training class and was shocked that she was accepted. Lissette gave it her all. She was diligent in her studies—never wavering in her passion and desire to become the first female motor officer in the Daytona Beach Police Department.

Lissette passed her pretest and was excited to let her sergeant know the results. "I could not believe it when I told him I passed, and all he could say was that I was 'too green and needed more time to grow and work on patrol.' It was a tough pill to swallow," Lissette said.

"But I sucked it up and told him I will do what I can, though I was obviously disappointed," Lissette recalled. Not too long after, Lissette was approached by her captain who asked her to move to the narcotics division, but she declined. "Thank you, sir, for the opportunity, but I really want to be a motor," she told him. Lissette became painfully aware that the motors typically fit a certain mold. "These guys were always tall, big guys and they looked tough," Lissette added. "While I was obviously not that, I knew I could hold my own; I refused to give up."

Lissette was no pushover and made sure she was not ignored by the command staff. When she heard about a motor officer position becoming available, Lissette was the first person to apply.

"Finally, my dream came true, and I was admitted to the training class to become an official motor officer; I was over the moon," Lissette recounted.

After Lissette completed her training, she got to know a colleague, Sergeant Rhodes, who believed in her ability and eventually became her mentor. He was also her surrogate father at the department. Lissette was determined to make him proud of her and prove that she could be just as tough and effective on the job as the guys. "The first three months were physically and mentally so draining," Lissette recalled. "Every day we would be on our bikes issuing tickets and riding around for hours. One day I called my mom crying and told her I did not think this job was for me. She said, 'Lissette, what do you mean? You worked too hard to get to where you are and you have to push through it.' I, of course, took her advice."

For nine years, Lissette was the only woman motor officer in the department. And everyone noticed. While on her motorcycle, Lissette would receive a wide range of responses from people who she came across at special events and others who she issued tickets to or even arrested. "I would get a mix of comments such as, 'You kick ass, girl, way to go!' Then there were others who had the audacity to ask me if I 'earned' the position. But over time I took those comments in stride and felt satisfaction when many of my colleagues said they regretted not believing in me," Lissette added.

Being a police officer—no matter if you are on a motorcycle or working in the homicide division—is emotionally taxing. No matter the training and learning to compartmentalize emotions, they are always close to the surface.

* * *

Lissette remembers an experience early in her law enforcement career that affected her for many years after the initial incident.

"There was a little boy who was chasing his brother in a church parking lot when his brother ran in the road and the little boy ran after him. He was hit by a car and died on the spot," Lissette recalled. "When I arrived at the scene, his mother was inconsolable; her husband was on a hunting trip in Canada and could not be reached. I stayed with the mom all day until her husband was contacted. It was so sad to see his brother mistakenly believe he was responsible for his sibling's death. While we are trained to be monotone when we talk to families of victims, and not get involved personally, in this case I could not. I decided to go to the funeral and make it personal. After so many of these tragedies, I decided to put myself in check and begin thinking correctly," Lissette explained.

Most law enforcement officers cite any situation involving children as among the most emotionally charged experiences. This was no different for Lissette. "When I was working at the Center and now as a police officer, I would see the same kids on the street and that was heartbreaking," said Lissette. "One of the kids in my program was living in a crack house, overdosed, and was found dead. After about eight years on the job, I was not becoming the person that stored things inside. I chose to talk to a counselor to bounce off my experiences, and make sure I had ways to cope with situations like these."

After nine years as a motor officer, Lissette was offered a new position within the department that she could not pass up. "They offered me a position in the Sex Crimes Unit where I would help sexual assault victims who were both children and adults," said Lissette. "We had to attend sex crimes training classes for two weeks to learn all the things we can and cannot do, especially with kids. For example, kids have a separate set of rights than adults and interviews are conducted differently. Children can only be interviewed three times with a child advocate present and in a controlled environment," she added.

There were a few situations in the Sex Crimes Unit that Lissette said affected her emotionally for years. "There was a young girl who was sexually assaulted by her mother's boyfriend when she was sleeping in her bed. She was only six years old and when she was interviewed, she described what happened as 'bugs' crawling on her. But when she woke up it was the mother's boyfriend, not the bugs who were sexually assaulting her," Lissette said.

Lissette said that before the trial, she handed the young girl a stuffed pig to try to calm her down. During the entire process, Lissette observed that her mother never hugged her even once and provided no emotional support. Lissette made sure that the courtroom was filled with enough law enforcement officers so the little girl would not see the offender. "I felt for this poor young girl. And the worst part was that the offender had been previously convicted of sexual assault on a minor but that could not be admitted in court. But I was relieved that he was convicted and sent to prison for a long time," Lissette said.

Another case that Lissette said had an impact involved a fellow law enforcement officer. It was a huge case for the unit and Lissette in particular. A seven-year-old girl was sexually assaulted by a retired deputy. "It was a big case when you have a deputy you are supposed to trust," Lissette said. "He was her neighbor and convinced her to 'do things' to him in the bathroom. I knew she could not make this up."

It infuriated Lissette that the deputy, who had just retired as a court bailiff, was a sick person and got away with his heinous crimes for so long.

There was another case Lissette was involved with as a member of the Sex Crimes Unit where she dealt with a serial rapist. "There was an adult case where the serial rapist talked in third person. He would say things to me such as, 'Lonzie Williams does not have sex with white women.' It was weird. The victim in this case was almost killed by Mr. Williams. While stabbing her, he narrowly missed her neck but instead slashed her mouth wide open. He also raped another woman, and his DNA was linked to the crime. Thankfully, he will spend the rest of his life in jail," said Lissette.

The next steppingstone in Lissette's career was in the Homicide Division. "You have to work your way up and be invited to be part of the unit," said Lissette. "I enjoyed my time there and felt good about being able to find closure for someone's family and give them the answers they needed," she said. "I want to find justice for victims and their families and make sure the criminals get what they deserve," she added.

One of Lissette's most memorable cases in the Homicide Division was that of Nelcie Tetley. She was a sixty-seven-year-old woman who had a previous boyfriend who had been killed. His corpse was dismembered and stuffed inside garbage bags on the banks of the Tomoka River in Ormand Beach. She convinced detectives that she did not kill him and blamed the murder on a serial killer named Gary Hilton. That was ten years before the next incident.

Lissette got involved in another murder committed by Nelcie that Lissette described as "the most gruesome" she has ever encountered. Lissette said that Nelcie was accused of killing her boyfriend inside his home. He was found with gunshot wounds to his head and chest. What they did not find were his arms and legs!

"Nelcie believed in witchcraft and so she not only shot my victim but after she shot him, drained the blood out of his body and scattered his limbs throughout the county," said Lissette. "She was clearly a very disturbed individual."

Initially, a male detective interviewed Nelcie, and Lissette could see she was a flirtatious, manipulative woman. She was having none of it. "Nelcie was the strangest person I have ever interrogated, and the most disturbed," Lissette said. "My victim was finally found ten days later—his arms and legs were about twenty miles away in De Leon Springs, and then we learned she had also killed another boyfriend. How is it that one woman could date two men and both die in the same way? Lissette wondered. "It was fascinating to watch her manipulate the lead detective, claiming she did not do it. I could see right through her. She was so playing him in the interview. When I entered the interrogation room, we did the good cop, bad cop technique. It was a long seven-month investigation, but I was thrilled that we finally had a warrant for her arrest," Lissette added. In 2018, a judge ordered Nelcie Tetley be jailed without bond and charged with first degree murder for killing her boyfriend and dismembering his body.

This case added another vexing question for Lissette. How could she tell the victim's family that their adult son was located and was dead, but his body parts were missing, in the most compassionate way? "I had many sleepless nights wondering what else I could have done better to help the family deal with such devastating news," said Lissette. "I did the best I could, but it still weighed on me for a long, long time."

But the most challenging homicide Lissette was ever involved with was also the most personally devastating.

"It was in December 2017, and I was working my homicide case when my mom called me crying hysterically," Lissette recalled.

"Your brother was just arrested for killing someone," her mother said.

"Are you sure?" Lissette asked her mom, knowing in her gut that Mark was guilty.

"I called the Sheriff's Office of Okeechobee and asked to speak to the person in charge. I said, 'This is a homicide investigator from the Daytona Beach Department, and I believe you have my brother in custody. What can I do to help you?' He confirmed that my brother, Mark, took someone's life," Lissette said.

Lissette recalled that the detective was a "nice" guy and told her he would share all the information with her and her family members. He even let Lissette listen to her brother's drug-induced and rambling 911 call. "I had to convince my mom that he actually did this because she was always in denial that Mark had a problem. I said, 'Mom, this is not your fault. Mark made his own choices and we all have choices in life.' I remember listening to the tape and Mark taunting the cops that he was not coming out of the house until the sheriff came. 'You come and get me,' he told them. It was a very emotional time, and I had to explain to Mom what was going on with Mark without being in a cop mode," said Lissette.

Mark was high on methamphetamine at the time the murder occurred. He was sharing a house with another male and female. He rigged the house with cameras because as a meth addict, he was paranoid. Apparently, there was an argument and Mark cut his roommate's face, and when the female entered the room, he stabbed her in the chest. She managed to walk out of the house but died after she bled out on the front lawn.

"I was embarrassed as a homicide detective, but I made sure my supervisor and chief were aware of what happened right away. They were wonderful and told me they would do whatever I needed. But it took me a few days before I discussed the murder with my squad," Lissette recalled. "I made an appointment with Dr. Tim, my counselor, to make sure I was able to separate my work and personal life. It goes to show that no matter where you come from or who is in your family, you choose your own path. I was the first one to go to college and receive a master's degree in criminal justice. This is the path I chose. Mark made his own choices and had to pay the price."

Over time Lissette came to terms with Mark's incarceration and life sentence for murder. Her mother realized she did the best she could and dealt with Mark's final, heinous act of violence in her own way.

After working in the Homicide Division for five years, Lissette decided to apply for a supervisor position in the Motor Division. She was promoted but needed to be placed back on street patrol for one year as part of the promotion requirements.

As it turned out, a position opened unexpectedly and Lissette was asked to take over as the supervisor. "I was thrilled to be back where my career all began," said Lissette. "Now as a supervisor I am in charge of a twelve-officer traffic unit that plans traffic logistics for special events [and] then facilitates and executes those plans," she said.

And unlike other communities across the country that have poor relationships with law enforcement, Daytona Beach Police Department has the support of the community—both White and Black. "We are blessed to have great community support and great leadership," said Lissette.

This was especially on display after the Jason Raynor murder. Officer Jason Raynor was shot in the face in June 2021, while responding to a suspicious incident. He died from his injuries on August 17, 2021, surrounded by his family. "It was devastating for all of us, but our community supported us one hundred percent," Lissette said. "The community came together, and it was so touching. We have strong relationships that we have built for twenty years. They are caring and decent people that have become part of our lives as well; we are truly blessed," said Lissette.

What is next for this motor cop turned motor cop supervisor? "I hope I can continue to be a role model for younger females. It makes me feel great knowing that we now have many female motor officers in other counties. I know I broke the mold seventeen years ago, but I earned it and so did the other women on their motorcycles who are keeping their communities safe," said Lissette.

Lissette, in her free time, organizes fundraisers to advocate for non-profit organizations that help fallen officer's families. She also supports the Special Olympics and helps organize motorcycle rides that also support fallen officers' families. She even has her own non-profit—Team Daytona Law Enforcement Charities—that is her way of giving back to her law enforcement brothers and sisters, whom she credits for giving her the experience of a lifetime.

"People often ask me how I achieved so much in such a brief time? I have to thank my mom, and I do all the time. She showed me that I could achieve anything I wanted if I put my mind to it. Even being a motor cop," said Lissette.

Two

HOMETOWN HERO

Last night I sat him up behind the wheel and said son take a good look around. This is your hometown.

—Bruce Springsteen

I F HOME IS WHERE THE HEART IS, THEN EVAN WEAVER HAS BUILT A FOUNDA-
tion on trust, compassion, and a belief that everyone deserves a second chance—even the bad guys. He should know. He has grown up
watching prostitutes coming and going from the house next door, seeing his
friends hooked on crack cocaine and heroin, and wondering why his neighborhood was so messed up. Instead of wanting to get out of Dodge as soon
as he turned eighteen, Evan decided to stay. To proudly put on the uniform
of an Allentown police officer and change his hometown for the better.

Evan was born in 1979 in the City of Allentown, Pennsylvania, the
third largest city in the state. It is also the place where the Liberty Bell was
hidden from the British during the American Revolutionary War. Over the
years, like many of America's inner cities, population migrations changed
the demographics as people moved out of the city and into the suburbs.

As a result, families such as Evan's lived in what he called "a lower
middle-class" neighborhood that, unfortunately, was located in one of
Allentown's high crime and drug infested areas. Evan and his family lived in
a small row home on Lumber Street with some unusual neighbors. "It was
quite a while until I learned what a prostitution house was," Evan said. "We
lived right next door, and I remember hearing the term, but I did not know

what it meant. All the women were very friendly to me and one day I was so curious, I asked my mom what prostitutes are and what do they do?"

Evan's mother explained what prostitutes did for a living. "I asked my mom: Why would anyone do that just to make money? Couldn't they get another job? I could see by her expression that was an uncomfortable question for her to answer," he added.

As Evan got older, he realized that most of the people on his block were using drugs. By the time he left for college, his was the only original family that remained. "It was a rough neighborhood, and violent activity was on the rise. Our house and others were shot at more times than I could count. It got to a point where my parents realized they just had to get out," Evan said.

The Weaver family moved to West Allentown. His father was an industrial radiographer and worked for many years at Bethlehem Steel. His mother not only had four children of her own—including Evan's younger brother, Andrew, and his older sisters, Tamera and Demitria, but was a foster parent as well. She originally provided foster care for children without disabilities, but realized there was a need to help children with physical and/ or mental health challenges. "My mom took care of a baby named Chris from Philadelphia, who had severe brain damage. Then came Tony, who had cerebral palsy. Eventually, my parents legally adopted both boys," said Evan.

Evan did very well academically despite growing up in a rough neighborhood. At William Allen High School, he was in advanced placement classes in science and anatomy and was always good with his hands. So much so that he thought he might want to be a carpenter. "I thought I would like to be in the trades, but my mom would not hear of it and said I had to go to college. So, I attended DeSales University, which was a Catholic university, and majored in criminal justice," Evan recalled. "But growing up I also thought I would want to go into the military because both my dad and uncle were in the army and navy. I remember as a young kid I would run around the house in fatigues and try to practice shooting things with my toy guns."

Evan eventually realized that he wanted to have a career where he could serve and help others. "What I saw growing up was eye-opening," Evan said. "There were so many drugs around. One of my friends actually became a criminal. During a robbery, he shot a woman. That is when it really hit home that I needed to do something about crime right here in my hometown."

After graduation, Evan began the application to become an Allentown police officer. "It was a tough process, so I sent applications to both the

Pennsylvania State Police and the Allentown Police Department. That was right before 9/11 and after my graduation from DeSales," Evan said.

During the waiting period, Evan joined one his friends who worked in a heating, ventilation, and air conditioning (HVAC) business, and he became certified. To earn extra money, he also worked at the local Home Depot. Finally, in 2003, Evan was contacted by both the Allentown Police Department and the Pennsylvania State Police and was asked to take the required tests. "I ranked in the top one hundred out of 2500 candidates in the state test and was number two out of sixty for Allentown. I went to the oral interview for the Pennsylvania State Police, and at the time I was only twenty-two years old and had never interviewed for a job in law enforcement before. My interview skills were not very polished," he said. "My interview was in Center City Philadelphia. I was so nervous. I remember trying to find the building and running red lights to make sure I got there on time," Evan added.

Evan's oral interview was scored in the low eighties, so between his low score and other candidates having prior military experience, where they were awarded extra points, he was knocked out of the running. But Evan was not the kind of person who was easily discouraged.

Evan's uncle had a suggestion that seemed to make sense. He persuaded Evan to apply for the US Marines Officer Candidate School. Evan agreed, and he began the process of recruiting and testing when he received a call that would cement the trajectory of his life.

"I received a call from the Allentown assistant police chief, and he asked me if I was still interested in becoming a police officer. I thought: *Is he serious? Of course, I want to do that.*" Evan rushed over to police headquarters, completed the necessary paperwork, and, in 2003, passed the physical test and was hired.

Despite Evan having to skip the first few days at the Police Academy in June because he was the chaperone for his foster brothers during his parents' planned trip to Colorado, he made it back just in time to not miss too much of the program.

In October 2003, Evan graduated along with twenty-two other young men and women. He was assigned to the second platoon and was fortunate to have several top-notch supervisors. Since there were so many new officers, the city did not have enough badges to go around. In addition, the uniforms were light blue in color and looked just like those of a postal worker. "I felt ridiculous in what I thought would be an impressive police uniform,"

Evan lamented. "And to top it off, they changed our shirt patches to one of our Center City monuments and it looked like a phallic symbol. No one thought I was for real, and one person even asked me where his mail was. Thank goodness one of my supervisors was kind enough to give me his patrol badge and I finally began to feel legitimate."

It was six months before Evan was properly outfitted with his own badge as an Allentown police officer, and it would be several years before the city changed the uniforms back to a more traditional dark blue. His days of looking like an armed postal worker were over.

Evan knew the City of Allentown like the back of his hand, which made his training easier. He was able to focus on learning how to interact with citizens and police the city instead of having to learn his way around town.

The training program lasted four weeks and then Evan became a floater with his assignments changing every day. At the time, the police department had only eight squad cars and two paddy wagons; Evan had no partner at the time. "Center City still had a high crime and high drug rate but oddly enough that is where I was most comfortable. It was where I was born and grew up so for me, community policing was as natural as breathing," said Evan.

Evan always took initiative in his policing. He was a present figure in all the high crime neighborhoods and spent time talking to people as well as making successful arrests. "The changes in these neighborhoods made me feel terrible. One of the problems with the word 'neighborhood' is that the people who lived in those areas for a long time were being pushed out due to the rising crime. When they finally moved out, the people who moved in were transient and did not care about the neighborhood. They only lived there for a few months and ended up being evicted for not paying their rent. That was the end of the sense of community," Evan explained.

One of Evan's greatest skills was his empathy and ability to talk to people from all levels of society—people who for a host of reasons found themselves living in poverty and despair.

"I always enjoyed interacting with people. Every day I would walk the streets and let the residents get to know and see me. There are a lot of good people who, unfortunately, are overrun by the bad people who live right next door—people who are poor and have no money to move to a safer neighborhood. Having been there myself I felt like I owed them. The bad guys know I am always there, and they have to contend with me," Evan remarked.

Evan had such a ubiquitous street presence and trust among the residents he served that he became more like a family member than a law enforcement officer. "People fed me wherever I went, and I did eat a lot of Spanish food, which is one of my favorites. The neighbors knew the value of having a strong police presence and they always let us know we were valued and welcomed," Evan said.

Despite the goodwill of a majority of the residents of Center City Allentown, Evan's job was to get guns off the streets and make sure drugs, prostitution, and gang activity were in check. He realized early on in his career that being complacent could be dangerous and cost him his life. "One of the dangers of being complacent is assuming that every encounter is routine. As soon as you do, you will fail to anticipate what could be a very terrible outcome," he said. "You can literally conduct one hundred traffic stops with no issues and get lulled into that sense of comfort. Then the 101st traffic stop goes sideways and you are not ready. Those are the ones that end badly," Evan added.

For example, there was a time early in Evan's career where he conducted a routine traffic stop with an unanticipated outcome. Evan's initial encounter was positive, and nothing appeared more unusual about this traffic stop than any others in which he had been involved. The stop occurred in one of the city's federal housing projects, which was a high crime and drug area. "After we finished up the initial part of the stop, and I gave the driver his documents back, I asked him if we could search the vehicle. He told me that he did not have any guns or drugs in the vehicle and gave me permission to do a search," Evan said. In addition to the driver, there were two other males inside who Evan recalled were polite. He assumed he would find nothing, issue a ticket, and be on his way. It turned out that was the furthest from the truth. "My senses that would alert me to danger were down, and I assumed I would find nothing. I could not have been more wrong."

As Evan was patting down one of the males, the man's pleasant demeanor abruptly changed. He became agitated, and Evan realized he might have given him the benefit of the doubt too soon. He had lost his edge. "I had the male up against the back of the vehicle. I found drugs in his pocket during the first pat down. I handcuffed him and had him lean over the trunk of the car. Every time I would push his upper body forward, he would stand back up. It turned out he had a handgun tucked into his waistband and drugs in his pocket," Evan recalled.

After Evan and his partner removed the two males from the vehicle and searched the car, they located a second handgun under the seat where one of the males was sitting with a sizeable amount of cocaine. They handcuffed all three of the males, and a warrant check revealed that two of them had outstanding warrants. One was from Puerto Rico where he was wanted for a homicide. A simple traffic stop resulted in confiscating two guns, a substantial amount of drugs, and the arrest of two violent actors.

It was a red flag for the rookie Allentown police officer. "That situation I put myself in really shook me. It was a wake-up call. I do not think I ate for two days. I was so disappointed in myself for being so nonchalant. I had this pit in my stomach. I knew I had put myself in a position where if the guy wanted for homicide decided he was not going to be arrested, he would have the jump on me. If he decided to start shooting, I would not have had time to react and he would have won the gun fight," Evan recalled.

"There is nothing that is routine in our line of work and nice can quickly turn into not so nice. At any moment if I were off guard like I was, I could have been shot. This life-changing moment really opened up my eyes," Evan said.

Evan made it a point, with every interaction, to expect the worst; otherwise he would fall into complacency. He developed his own strategy for anticipating every eventuality, and then tried to take control of the situation by catching the bad guys off guard and making them feel relaxed in an effort to have a more positive outcome. "If I can arrest someone without a fight and go on my way, I am happy. Part of our de-escalation training is to talk to actors and convince them to comply with minimal force. I want to avoid having to go hands-on and fight guys because that leads to injuries and exposures. A lot of the people we deal with, especially in high drug and crime areas, are using drugs, shooting up heroin, and have not showered for days," Evan explained. "The heroin users will shoot up and defecate wherever they are—on the sidewalk, or on the floor of an abandoned house. The last thing I want to do is have an exposure to blood or other bodily fluids and bring home any diseases to my family."

Proactive policing was one way Evan could locate people who were up to no good. "Because I spent so much time patrolling the same neighborhoods, I had a good eye for people who were out of place," said Evan. "I would see people loitering on the block or on the corner, and I would give them a verbal warning. If I came around a second time, and they were still there, I would park my car and address them. I arrested a lot of actors that way."

Evan said that these addicts and bad actors would try to take over a block and turn it into an open-air drug market. "At the time, we had a lot of gang members in the city. The Bloods, the Crips, Latin Kings, and other groups that had a foothold in various parts of the city," Evan recounted. "We were fortunate enough to have really dedicated officers and assistance from other law enforcement agencies to combat the crimes being committed. All of that hard work and perseverance paid off. Numerous gang members were arrested and sent to state and federal prison for their crimes. And it decimated the gangs. Unfortunately, they still exist, but they are disorganized and no longer have the impact they once had on crime in the city."

Despite the inherent dangers of being a police officer, Evan would continue being aggressive and proactive in his policing and, unfortunately, this led to Evan experiencing several close calls.

There was the time he was patrolling the Seven Hundred block of Turner Street, which was a block away from an elementary school that was in the process of letting students out for the day. He noticed a male who had been loitering in the area for over an hour. Evan had to respond to a number of calls during that time but finally had a break and was able to address the male. He stepped out of his car and, as he was questioning the man, got conflicting answers. Evan realized he did not belong in the area and had no valid reason for being there.

As Evan began to conduct a pat down, he located crack cocaine in the male's pocket. He had a feeling he was going to run because he was actively looking around and trying to position himself in a way that he had a clear path to escape. "During encounters like this, I would make sure I kept a hand on the actor's shirt. That way, if he decided to flee, I would have a way to gain control. I was right; the male started to run but he did not get very far," Evan recalled. "As I took him to the ground and attempted to gain control of him, I noticed another male aggressively approaching us from down the block. He started yelling at me as he came closer. I assumed he was a friend of the male I was attempting to hand cuff. At the same time, I remember hearing the distinctive roar of motorcycles approaching. The group stopped right next to where I was trying to control that actor. As we were on the ground, the guys on the motorcycles got off their bikes and came towards us."

They all stopped next to the sidewalk where the male was actively resisting arrest. "In that moment I was alone and still trying to gain control of the actor's arms. Just then I noticed a second actor on the sidewalk approaching me. Now, I had to contend with six guys who just got off their motorcycles and I was unable to radio for assistance because of the resisting actor. I yelled, 'Everyone, get back!' That is when one of the guys on the motorcycles screamed, 'We're on the job!' I knew this meant that he was also a police officer. *What a relief*," Evan remembered thinking.

Ironically, the motor officers just happened to be driving across the country from California and were members of the California Highway Patrol. When the friend of the resisting male saw that Evan had some serious help, he turned and fled. With the help of the other officers, they were able to handcuff the belligerent male. "That was my lucky day," Evan admitted.

Another situation that left Evan with serious physical injuries happened in 2008. He was dispatched to help contain a loose pit bull. "I am a dog lover, so I wanted to do my best and secure the dog. I was able to feed the dog beef jerky and get him on a leash safely. Typically, we do not transport animals in our police cars. We notified the local Humane Society, but on this day they were not available, so our only option was to transport the dog in the back of the paddy wagon," Evan recalled.

While Evan was waiting for the paddy wagon to arrive, he placed the dog in the rear seat of his police car. He seemed friendly and Evan continued to pacify him by feeding him more beef jerky. (He remembers calling his wife telling her that the dog was friendly and that he was in the back of the car enjoying his treat.)

"Once the paddy wagon arrived, I took the dog out of my car and walked him over to the rear of the wagon. He still had a pleasant demeanor and waited patiently for me to open the rear door of the wagon. I pulled the leash up and he jumped right in. Then, he turned around and jumped back down and this happened at least two or three times," Evan said. "My plan was that I would get in the wagon and walk him to the front of the holding area. He followed me and sat down and was a good boy—or so I thought. As I reached down to remove his leash, I felt like I was hit in the face with a brick!"

Evan dropped to the floor when the dog jumped up and hit him straight in the mouth. His bite was ferocious and his jaw wrapped tightly around Evan's face. "I found myself lying on top of the dog and every time the dog tried to shake his head, I could feel my face tearing apart," Evan said.

Evan grabbed the dog and shoved his fingers into his mouth. He eventually released Evan's face but clamped right back down on his fingers. "Now I had my face out of the dog's mouth, but both hands were still stuck in there. I felt the dog's teeth bearing down on my lip and his bite was so severe that I fell to the ground, blood dripping from my mouth. The dog bit me so hard that it drove my head into the roof of the wagon. He drug me down to the ground and the fight was on."

"My partner, who was driving the wagon, jumped into action to help get the dog off of me. The dog finally released my hands and my partner and I exited the wagon. Out of nowhere the dog turned around and immediately jumped out of the wagon and started running toward us. My partner ended up shooting the dog, which was sad but a necessary thing to do," Evan said.

As Evan lay bleeding on the ground from his face and hands, residents came out of their homes yelling at the officers, "Dog murderers!" Evan was rushed to the hospital where he had a concussion, two broken teeth on the left side of his face, and most of his nails punctured on both of his hands. He also needed forty stitches inside his mouth. "Even though I was torn up by that dog, I was upset that he was shot. I always loved dogs, but after this incident I was hesitant to let any dogs get close to me for quite a while after that. I am lucky though because my wife, Michelle, is a therapist by training, so she helped me get over my fear," said Evan.

And then there was another traumatic event that still haunts Evan to this day.

He was dispatched to a home in Allentown, Pennsylvania, where a mother had arrived home to find her daughter murdered in the basement. She was just eighteen years old. She looked like she had engaged in a struggle and it was later determined that she was strangled to death. "I found myself standing in the basement of the house, trying to console a mother who had just found her daughter deceased. It was a struggle to maintain my demeanor as a police officer and hide my emotions," Evan recalled. "The image of that innocent victim was burned in my brain, and I can still vividly recall how she looked; I am sure I will never forget," he added.

It turned out that her sister's boyfriend strangled her; the scene was gruesome, as homicides usually are. "It was heartbreaking for me to see this young girl who was going to school to become a dental assistant end up this way. We found her in the coal chute and what a horrible way to die. Her murder sticks with me even to this day," Evan recalled.

In fact, for years after the homicide, anytime Evan was driving in his squad car or his own vehicle, when he saw a woman who looked like the young victim, he would freeze. "I kept seeing her lifeless body in women who I thought looked like her. And I had more than a few tough nightmares, but Michelle would talk me through them as she has always done in the past," Evan said.

According to Evan, spouses of police officers do not get enough credit. "We are exposed to horrific incidents every day. Death and despair—these are the things we do not want to share with our family. This repeated trauma can cause a great deal of friction at home. It is incredibly hard to talk to your wife and explain what you have seen or done that day. Our wives have to indirectly deal with the same trauma we deal with but they provide us with a sense of normalcy and comfort," Evan explained.

Once Evan and Michelle had children, Evan's policing philosophy in terms of his personal safety changed. "Before I had kids, I never thought about how the situations I put myself in would impact others around me," said Evan. "My physical safety was never really a thought. I would go to every call and run the worst case scenarios through my head so that I would be prepared, but I would expect the best. I never gave a thought to what would happen if I were killed. I knew that it was a possibility; I just never really thought about it."

"It is a hard way to go through life, anticipating the worst-case scenario every time you have an interaction with someone. It weighs on you and can impact your home life. When I finally had kids, I understood what it meant to be needed. I realized I needed to be there for them. I had no choice but to think about my mortality. I did not want my kids to grow up without a dad. This is a heavy weight on my shoulders but it reinforces all of my training to never, ever be complacent," Evan added.

The stress that law enforcement professionals face is palpable and one of the reasons Evan believes that law enforcement officers have high rates of divorce, suicide, or alcoholism. It can be difficult for them to find the proper outlet to deal with the trauma they have experienced. Physical injuries are always an occupational hazard, but the emotional tolls can be equally devastating.

* * *

In 2009, Evan had another traumatic experience and nearly lost his life while trying to arrest a suspect. "As I was trying to arrest a male, instead of him complying, he tried to run me over! I literally went for a ride on the hood of his car for about two hundred feet before I was able to jump off. It was physically devastating because it left me with several herniated discs in my back," Evan recalled. "They were so severe that I had to ask my wife to help me put on my pants, socks, and shoes. My doctors wanted to operate, but they said I would only have a fifty/fifty chance of improvement, so I decided to go with physical therapy instead. Fortunately, with many months of therapy I was able to make a near full recovery," he added.

When Evan first became a police officer with the Allentown Police, he met members of the Emergency Response Team (ERT)—this is the same as a SWAT Team. "These guys are the cream of the crop and are the people that the police call when things go really wrong. I wanted to be one of these guys, and despite my injuries and setbacks, I was thrilled to be selected to be a member of the ERT," Evan said. As a member of the ERT, Evan honed his skills clearing a room, breaching a door, and took part in intense shooting practice to make sure the shots were accurate, and the rounds went where they should.

On February 14, Valentine's Day, Evan, his wife, and two children were eating dinner together at a local restaurant. Before they left, Evan was aware that he would probably be called soon to serve a warrant. As if on cue, the phone rang and the call that Evan was anticipating arrived. "I told my wife that I am sorry but had to go. She knew all too well that even on Valentine's Day, me getting a work call was part of the job. But for my oldest daughter that was another story. I was surprised at her response when she said: 'Daddy, do not get killed.' I gave her a kiss and told her I would be fine. Then I told my wife and kids how much I loved them and would see them later."

Evan left the restaurant and headed to an apartment a few blocks away where a homicide victim was found stuffed into a garbage can. She was shot multiple times. It was believed that the homicide may have occurred at the victim's residence. Members of the Criminal Investigations Unit were able to secure a search warrant. At the time, they were not sure if the suspect was in the apartment.

Evan was able to locate a key for the apartment, and as they made entry into the building, they found the victim's apartment. With the key in his hand, Evan placed it in the deadbolt lock and opened the door. He came up close and personal with the barrel of a gun.

"The male grabbed the door and ripped it open and we were met with a rifle barrel and a pistol barrel. I drew my pistol and fired twelve rounds into the male. I could literally feel the heat coming from the barrel. The percussion of the gun shots was jarring," Evan said.

Evan realized there was another apartment door directly across from the suspect's door. "I banged on the window from the outside to get the residents' attention and then pulled them out to safety. Luckily, none of them was harmed," he continued. The officers negotiated with the man for hours before they breached the exterior wall and took the man into custody. When they searched the apartment, they found numerous guns placed in multiple locations to ambush any officers who came through the door. The perp pleaded guilty to killing his girlfriend and received sixty years in prison.

Though Evan has had his share of incidents and arrested hundreds of criminals, he still has empathy for those he locks up, despite their heinous acts. "I feel like I am the same guy I was when I began my career twenty years ago. I still go to work trying to help people and that makes me feel good. I do not feel good locking up people because I know that you change the dynamics of their families. A kid will have no mom or dad, and families will be torn apart; it is a powerful responsibility to be entrusted with someone else's freedom, and I do not take it lightly. That being said, if I can lock up a truly bad person, help a kid who is in a bad situation, or help someone who is the victim of domestic violence, I feel good about that. If I can help prevent someone from being victimized, I feel like I am serving my purpose," Evan explained.

In 2011, when Evan had been recently assigned to the Vice and Intelligence Unit, he was involved in a lawsuit—something he never dreamed would ever happen. It stemmed from an incident that had occurred years before.

It was a Sunday morning, and Evan was on patrol near a busy 7-Eleven store, where every day he would stop, buy a Diet Coke, and talk to the employees. Evan was dispatched to that exact 7-Eleven to deal with two black males who were smoking crack right in front of the store. As Evan pulled into the parking lot, he immediately observed the males standing in front of the store smoking crack out of a glass crack pipe.

He exited his police car and approached the males, ordering them to place their hands on the rear of his police car and on the trunk. "I started patting the one male down and found crack cocaine in his pocket. As soon as I did, the male decided to make a run for it, but I used my tried and true technique that I have used a hundred times to subdue him. I grabbed his shirt, but the male had me in tow! Finally, I was able to get him on the ground, even though he continued to resist arrest," Evan recalled.

About one minute later, another officer arrived, and the two officers were able to handcuff the male.

During the struggle, the contents of Evan's shirt pockets were strewn across the parking lot. The second male came to Evan's aid, and to his surprise, picked up Evan's belongings while he patiently waited for the first male to be detained. Evan arrested the first male for possessing crack cocaine and it was also found that he had an outstanding warrant for his arrest.

Months later, and to Evan's disbelief, he was sued for $10 million claiming he violated the male's civil rights. The plaintiff claimed Evan violently threw him on the ground and called him racial slurs. There was a full federal trial, and thanks to the city's closed-circuit cameras outside the 7-Eleven, there was absolute proof that the incident never happened the way the male claimed. The jury deliberated for only thirty minutes, even though the trial lasted about three days; Evan was cleared of all charges.

But the incident left emotional scars despite Evan being exonerated. "For a while I did not want to be at work, and I was angry," Evan recalled. "People told me not to let it get me down. But it pulled at my heart strings because I spent seven years working with minorities and doing the best I could do protect everyone. This lawsuit really hurt."

Following the lawsuit, in 2012 Evan began working with the FBI Violent Crime Task Force, which identifies and apprehends violent drug dealers, which often fight over their turf and drug money. A less dangerous assignment, according to Evan: "Patrol officers have the most dangerous job because they have no idea what kind of people they will encounter during routine traffic stops, for example. Even though I have been through some tough situations, I still have excitement knowing I am doing an important job. There is nobility in doing it well."

But there are those moments when the reality of the job hit particularly hard. "I have been called a lot of things in my career, and generally I let them roll off my back. But one of my kids recently asked me, 'Daddy, why do people hate cops? What are you doing that people do not like you?' That hurt. How do you tell your kids you are not the enemy?" Evan lamented.

Law enforcement officers like Evan experience many traumas, but talking about their feelings with family, friends, and professionals is critical for their mental health and well-being. "I am lucky our department is very good about providing officers with help through counseling after traumatic events. They encourage open discussion and officers feel like they can speak freely and talk about any issues bothering them," Evan explained.

"This is the best job I have ever had, and I am not discouraged or have any animus about the state of policing today. I know things will change for the better. I am still proud of my hometown, and it means the world to me. If I have helped just one person lead a good and safe life here, I have done my job," Evan concluded.

Three

FROM FOOTBALL TO A SQUAD CAR

Success isn't measured by money or power or social rank. Success is measured by your discipline and inner peace.

—Mike Ditka

I
T MAY APPEAR INCONGRUOUS THAT A FORMER PROFESSIONAL FOOTBALL player would leave the NFL and take a job with a local police department. Why would someone who was treated like a superstar choose to tackle almost insurmountable issues between the police and the local residents they serve? Surprisingly, there are many athletes trading in their pads and helmets for shields and guns. For Deitan Dubuc, the choice was an easy one. His team of men and women in blue has scored off the field—fighting crime and protecting the citizens of Minneapolis in the process, despite a host of challenges.

Deitan Dubuc had quite an unusual childhood. He was born in Montreal, Canada, in 1977 and was the middle child among four other siblings—each was one year apart except the last two, who were three years apart. Interestingly, Deitan was the only one of the Dubuc children that was born in a hospital. Why? Because his family were members of a very restrictive religious cult called the Mission of the Holy Spirit. Deitan's parents were born into the cult and though they had issues with its teachings, they still decided to remain.

The Mission of the Holy Spirit was founded in 1913 in Quebec and is based on the teachings of Eugène Richer dit La Flèchei. Followers believe

27

Richer was the third person of the Holy Spirit. They ascribed supernatural powers to him, primarily reincarnation. Those who did not believe, according to the Mission's tenets, were condemned to hell as vermin. They also forced women to give birth at home and never wear jewelry or makeup. Unbelievably, they actually told followers that the earth was not round, but pear-shaped. "Even as a little kid I knew these people were different," said Deitan. "For example, they encouraged young people to get married at four-teen years old, barely old enough to make rational decisions let alone consider marriage."

Deitan's father was the oldest of eleven children and his mother the third of nine. "On my dad's side they all had lots of kids and at the latest count I have more than seventy cousins, all living in Canada. And among the most bizarre things about this cult is that mostly everybody has the same name, which is really crazy," Deitan said. Fortunately, his name was not that popular, and as a result, Deitan has only one cousin and one uncle with the same name.

"The other weird thing about being a child growing up in a cult is that on the one hand you know what you are seeing is strange, but on the other, it is all that you know. We were indoctrinated to believe that no one person can shine," Deitan said. "In fact, when other cult members would clip a story from the local paper about me when I played football, the Mission elders would hang it on the community bulletin board writing something next to the article such as, 'This is an example of what not to do.' It was all about conforming."

Every Sunday, Deitan and his family attended a Mission makeshift church which was located on one floor of a commercial building in Montreal. "They would tell us we could not play with 'the people of the world on Sunday.' *What was that supposed to mean?* I remember thinking, *are they nuts?* Dad and mom were not exemplary members of the cult, and they recognized that the cult was not adapting to societal change, which was why they allowed us to make the decision to stay or to leave the cult. My siblings and I had the realization that at some point we had to get out," Deitan recalled.

Deitan was homeschooled by several of his aunts on his father's side. They were not just relatives but also accomplished musicians and educators—many of whom had advanced degrees. In the sixth grade—and to Deitan's dismay—he received failing grades. "I could not believe I allowed myself to fail, but I did," Deitan said.

"When we were homeschooled, we had to travel to my aunt's house, which was miles away. We had to walk across a bridge, take a bus and subway for thirty minutes, and finally walk a few more blocks to her house. Leaving us on our own was not the best decision on my mom's part, but with all us kids around, I think she just needed a break," he said.

The long journey of the Dubuc children to school presented a host of problems. Regardless of the weather—snow, rain, or temperatures reaching thirty below zero—their parents never dropped them off. It was the beginning of experiencing the school of hard knocks for Deitan and his siblings.

"We saw things that no kids should have to at such an early age. Like perverts," Deitan said. "There was this pervert, who we could see had mental health issues, who liked my sister and would follow us to school and give her candy. He was always trying to get my sister's attention, and we soon figured out that we could get candy too, just by telling my sister what we wanted. When he would come around, she would add our candy choices to the list and just like that we got our top choices. Having to figure out things and problem solve was one benefit of being on our own; it would come in handy as we got older," Deitan recalled.

* * *

The Dubuc family eventually moved to Laval Island when Deitan was one year old. It sounds like an ocean oasis but, in reality, Laval Island is a city in Quebec bordered by two rivers. It is referred to as "Jesus Island" because in 1699 it was granted to the Society of Jesus and named after Francois de Montmorency Laval, the first Roman Catholic Bishop of Canada.

Laval Island had a public school named Sainte-Marguerite, and this was the first time Deitan and two of his siblings attended a brick-and-mortar facility and were not homeschooled. But Deitan soon felt like an outcast. "It was hard to connect to some of the people because they grew up very differently and were not as independent and self-sufficient. I also struggled with many of the school restrictions that I felt were ridiculous, such as having to go across the street with crossing guards, as an example," Deitan recalled. Deitan said that in Montreal he and his siblings could cross the streets wherever and whenever they wanted—that was the norm.

Because Deitan and his siblings were unfamiliar with life outside of their cult bubble, there were times when their social naiveté was obviously on display. Such as the time his youngest brother sat next to a woman on the bus wearing a long, amber-colored fur coat. "When he sat next to the lady, he noticed her coat and how soft it looked and so he took his hand and started rubbing it up and down her sleeve. He never saw a coat like this in his life. She felt his hand on her arm and just smiled, realizing he was just a young, naive boy," Deitan said.

The Dubuc children were left on their own at a time in their lives where they needed more guidance. To say they were mischievous would be an understatement. "Since we had so much time alone, we did some things that most kids would do when their parents were not around. We would slide down subway escalator rails, then run away. Then when we were in the subway car, we would open the door and stick our heads out. The conductor knew who we were and we would hear him yell at us over the intercom, 'Stop playing with the doors!'" Deitan recalled. They also took items from abandoned houses, picked up pennies to buy candy, then grabbed an extra handful, and enjoyed throwing bags of garbage over a bridge.

Deitan and his siblings found other mischievous ways to have fun, such as finding discarded neon lights in the trash and exploding them—creating quite a mess. But Deitan realized over the years that this lack of guidance enabled him to problem solve and find solutions on his own.

Deitan also had a talent for sports and played soccer for the city of Chomedey and in Fabreville leagues for eleven years beginning when he was six years old. His father was a hockey player in his youth and would have encouraged his son to do the same, if it were not so expensive. He also worked three jobs, and despite having only an eighth-grade education, did everything he could to provide for his family and support Deitan's propensity for athletics.

"I was always a fierce competitor," Deitan said. "Even when we were playing dodge ball when I was in the sixth grade, my teacher would punish me because she thought I was too rough and ruthless and did not listen to the rules. What did she expect? I was raised in a lower middle-class environment. But despite the fact that we had little money, my parents always made sure we never missed a meal. I guess you could say that social norms were not part of my DNA at that point."

In fact, not only was Deitan's family poor, but because of the cult's restrictive rules, they did not celebrate traditional holidays and Christmas presents were strictly forbidden. "When I was in public school, and we came back from the Christmas break, my friends would tell me about all of the gifts they received. As cult members we were not permitted to have a Christmas holiday or receive any gifts. I would lie and tell my friends about getting a video game, though I never played one in my life; I was totally embarrassed." Deitan said that though Christmas presents were not allowed, his parents still managed to skirt the rules and buy the children utilitarian items such as socks, boots, or gloves.

When Deitan was fourteen years old, he met his first girlfriend, Marie-Charles. She was thirteen and lived in what Deitan thought was a palace. They were inseparable; Deitan was in heaven. He had never seen anything like it and was transfixed by all of the new amenities of the large brick house with a lake view, such as an in-ground swimming pool and a paved patio. "Marie's house was amazing and had everything we did not in terms of material things. But what we did have in our family was each other," Deitan recalled.

The pair remained inseparable and, two years later when he was sixteen, Deitan's mother asked him if he wanted to remain in the cult. He did not hesitate to give her a definitive answer, simply telling her, "Peace out, mom; I am done!"

Deitan officially divorced himself from the cult he considered "weird" in 1993, though his oldest brother, Richer, remained because his wife's father was a priest.

Deitan was on cloud nine, officially starting a cult-free life, spending a lot of time at his girlfriend's house, going with her father on boat rides, swimming in their pool, eating at fancy restaurants, and even riding on their lawnmower. "Oh my gosh, this was heaven for me. It was the first time that I was taken to a fancy restaurant where I had no idea which utensil to start the meal with. Holy moly, I am this poor kid who did not have much—not even one Christmas present—and here I am surrounded by luxury," Deitan exclaimed. "Marie was so kind and bought me my very first Christmas present—a $350 Notre Dame Fighting Irish jacket. It was the best gift I ever received."

Deitan did very well living apart from the cult. He played soccer for a while but eventually found it boring. He had bigger dreams but no idea at that point in his life what they were.

But in his senior year of high school, Marie-Charles, a cheerleader for the football team, gave Deitan a novel idea. She asked him, "Have you ever considered playing football? Why not give it a try?" I told her, "I think I am too skinny to play football, but what the heck? I will have to ask my mom."

Despite Deitan's mother worrying that if he decided to play football he may incur lifelong injuries, she gave him her blessing anyway. At eighteen years old and in his senior year in high school, Deitan showed up at a football practice unannounced and brazenly asked the coach what position he should play.

"They gave me a jersey and pads, but I felt like an idiot because I had no idea how to put the pads in the girdle," Deitan lamented. "One of the guys on the team showed me how to do it. I was six foot four at the time and only 175 pounds, but I could run like a gazelle. The coach was losing his mind because he thought I was a super athlete but knew nothing about football. Oh my gosh, he was right!"

During one game, Deitan recalls his coach asking him to block the middle linebacker, but he had no idea what that was or where they lined up. At the end of the season, Deitan was contemplating trying out for the Spartitates du Vieux Montreal, the number one team in the College of Education General and Professional (CEGEP) League in Montreal. But he was told he was not good enough to play for them. That was the last time in Deitan's life that he allowed someone to tell him what he can and cannot do.

To his surprise, Deitan was approached by the head coach of the Spartitates du Vieux Montreal, Marc Santeere, and he invited Deitan to come and try out for the team. Fortunately, he accepted the invitation and gave football a thoughtful consideration.

"The guys I practiced with were animals," Deitan recalled. "One time [one guy] slapped me so hard on my stomach that you could see his handprint on my stomach for the entire day. But I knew right away that this is where I belonged."

Deitan was so motivated by playing with the best athletes in the city that he practiced every day and, despite having a fellow player head-butting his eye and sending him to the hospital where he received six stiches, he returned to practice, and he never missed another day. Deitan also found a mentor—a tight end from France who was six foot three and 250 pounds. At the time, Deitan was tall—six feet four but only 185 pounds. He worked Deitan hard, and Deitan was a willing and quite able student. Unfortunately, during a drill Deitan accidentally injured his mentor, who was the team's best player, and tore his ACL. The coach was furious. But there was no one else left in line so he made Deitan the starter. (The team lost in the semifinal that first year.)

But Deitan would not let the loss in the 1995 season deter him. "I worked out like a beast. I went from 185 to 205 pounds; I was ready to go," Deitan said. That next year they won the championship and during the third year they did it again; Deitan was over the moon when he made the all-star team two years in a row.

Coach Santeere, who was friends with Lloyd Carr, the head coach of Michigan, would take the best football player of Quebec to the University of Michigan summer football camp each year. While at camp, Deitan's raw talent caught the eye of college recruiters. Though, at twenty years old and not speaking any English—he had some serious challenges to overcome.

The quarterbacks, also attending the camp at Michigan, had to draw on the football what route they wanted Deitan to run since his English was so terrible. But the recruiters saw first-hand how fast Deitan could run, how well he caught balls, and how difficult it was for players to cover him. So, despite his language issues and only knowing a few words in English he picked up in Michigan, one of the coaches recognized his potential. He introduced Deitan to Coach Carr, and, to Deitan's surprise, the coach offered him a full scholarship. Coach Santeere was present in the meeting and translated every word for Deitan. "I asked the coach, 'Are you serious?' He said he was, and on the spot, I said, 'Okay, I will take it.' The coach said I should go home and ask my parents, and I told him that was not necessary since I was an adult. I could detect a smile on his face, which was fine to me."

When Deitan arrived back in Laval, reality set in. He had to learn English as soon as possible, and he was fortunate to find the perfect person to help him overcome his language obstacle. His name was Paul Menzies, and he was Deitan's teammate and friend from the Spartitates. Paul agreed to teach Deitan English, and Deitan was also taking lessons online to be able to pass the SAT—the exam needed to enter a college or a university. All that Deitan needed to be admitted to Michigan was a combined SAT score of 820. Though he did not understand all of the questions, Deitan beat the odds and received a combined score of 860. "I was so excited that I called the coach and told him my score, and he said I was in," said Deitan. "That was one of the best days of my life."

Deitan packed up his meager belongings and headed to Michigan in May 1998. The team had just won the won the national championship earlier that year and had the number one college football recruiting class. It was also the university where the winningest quarterback in NFL history, Tom Brady, got his start.

To say Deitan looked out of place would be an understatement. He had an unusual sense of fashion according to most American standards. He was teased mercilessly for wearing mid-thigh Daisy Duke shorts, a fanny pack, and black socks with white running shoes. "I thought I looked cool, because in Montreal that was the style, but clearly that was not the case in Michigan," Deitan said.

Steve Connelly, who worked for the team and the education department, was given the task to teach Deitan English so he would be ready when the school year began. Every day they worked hard, though Deitan kept writing words backwards, since in French a red apple would be called, "apple red," whereas in English it was the opposite. Deitan was frustrated when he went home two weeks prior to training camp. The football staff feared that Deitan would not return. After two weeks they sent Steve to Montreal to bring Deitan back to Michigan. Unbeknownst to them, Deitan already made the decision to come back and fulfill his dream.

"I went back to Ann Arbor because I am not a quitter. I asked Steve to arrange a meeting with the head of admissions, which he did on the spot. This is what I said to him: 'Sir, listen to me. I am an intelligent, industrious man with a language barrier, but I am not stupid. I will not fail, I promise you, and I will graduate. I know you are taking a chance on me, but you will not regret it.' To my surprise, he admitted me on the spot," Deitan recalled with great relief.

Deitan's college roommate as a freshman was Hayden Epstein. "He was seventeen and I was twenty-one, and he became my first actual English interpreter. Though we came from diverse backgrounds—Hayden, who was Jewish and was born in San Diego, and me, a kid from Montreal who was raised in a cult—we were close and are still friends to this day," said Deitan.

That first year on the football field was a rocky one for Deitan, including breaking his jaw. But he was not to be deterred. The coaches told Deitan that they wanted him to be a tight end. That position combines the jobs of both wide receivers and offensive linemen. They have to be large so they can be effective blockers. But at only 214 pounds, Deitan had a long way to go.

Deitan's first practice was a disaster, and he was embarrassed because he spent more time on the ground than on his feet, mainly because the defensive players were so strong and so good. He was dejected. "Even though I had four years under my belt, I felt no one believed in me, only me," said Deitan. But his determination paid off. He worked in the weight room every day, doing hundreds of reps to the point where he could not even push a leg press with even one pound on the machine. Michigan Strength and Conditioning Coach Mike Gittleson took Deitan as a project and broke him physically and mentally before building a bigger, stronger, and faster version of himself.

In his second year at Michigan, Deitan went from 214 to 272 pounds, consuming at least ten thousand calories a day, every day. In those first two years, he also mastered English and memorized all of his plays.

Things were going well for Deitan, and he was hopeful that he would eventually catch the eye of football scouts and be drafted by the NFL. After his fourth year at Michigan, he was brought into the head coach's office where he delivered the crushing news that they were not awarding him with his fifth-year option. In Deitan's mind, he thought it was a guarantee, which is why he left only one credit shy of graduating. This would have been horrific for Deitan since he purposely left that credit to play his fifth year. Fortunately, Deitan was told he had an opportunity to earn his scholarship a second time in the spring. "I worked like an animal, and I dominated everybody, and I was able to earn my scholarship for one more football season," Deitan said.

"Though I was up and down my fifth year, I knew that my time to shine would be at the NFL combine hosted at the University of Michigan. At the combine I ran the forty-yard dash in 4.57 seconds, bench pressed 225 pounds twenty-two times, and caught every ball thrown at me. I was dominant and exceeded all expectations," Deitan said. "The NFL recruiters asked around who this guy was, and I made sure they knew by the end of the workout," he added.

The NFL scouts did not have Deitan on their radar, so they asked him to run the forty-yard dash again, which he did in 4.58 seconds. That was his ticket to the NFL. Deitan signed with an agent, then later as a free agent with the Seattle Seahawks. He also graduated with a Bachelor of Arts degree in sports management and communications.

Deitan Dubuc, the skinny kid from a cult in Laval, was on his way.

But his career in the NFL would be short-lived and filled with injury and disappointment. "I loved being in the NFL, but I was fighting through a sprained MCL and trying to get back on the fifty-three-man roster," said

Deitan. But to his disappointment, he was released after the Seahawks lost two wide receivers to injuries in one week. After clearing the waiver—which is an NFL labor management deal that allows a football player's contract to be picked up by another NFL team—Deitan was picked up by the Carolina Panthers.

Deitan was excited to be part of the Panthers organization and was fortunate enough to be part of the 2004 Super Bowl team against Tom Brady. (The game with the infamous Janet Jackson wardrobe malfunction.)

After the Super Bowl, there were talks about Deitan being sent to NFL Europe—which was the NFL's minor football league that was in operation from 1991 to 2007. But because of his playmaking abilities that year, he was told that he would be invited to the 2004 training camp with the possibility of making the fifty-three-man roster. Unfortunately, during training camp the Panthers had several injuries on the offensive line and Deitan was released. After clearing waivers for a second time, the Houston Texans signed him. "For the first time ever, I played football angry because I knew I belonged in the NFL but my dream was cut short twice in one year," Deitan said. "But I had to do my job and pushed ahead as I always do."

During the Houston Texans scrimmage against the Miami Dolphins, Deitan was on fire. "I was doing really well, but then I blew out both my ankles on two different plays and was sidelined shortly thereafter; I was released two weeks later with an injury settlement. While I was devastated and missed the 2004 season, I returned to Canada in 2005 to play for the Edmonton Eskimos of the Canadian Football League," said Deitan.

Deitan won the Grey Cup Championship in 2005 with the Eskimos and believed that he could return to the NFL. But unfortunately, he was hurt once again in 2006. Deitan had to make a drastic career change when he realized his injuries were too severe to continue playing the sport he loved.

In 2007, Deitan fulfilled another of his lifelong dreams—to become a United States citizen. And he made the difficult decision to move on from football and to do something he had always wanted to do since he was ten years old: become a law enforcement officer.

In the interim, Deitan married his wife, Jenna, in 2002, and in 2004 the newlyweds moved to Minnesota, where his new wife had been born and raised. It would be a fresh start, and Deitan was excited about the future. After applying to the Minneapolis Police Department in June 2008, he was accepted and assigned to the Accelerated Cadet Program. By September, he had aced his exams at the academy and was sworn in as a Minneapolis police officer. He had come a long way from being a member of a weird religious cult, signed as a free agent in the NFL, and now a sworn law enforcement officer.

People have often asked Deitan, despite his numerous injuries, why he would give up a career with the NFL and choose to become a cop. The two seemed often incongruous, at least to everyone but Deitan. While he loved the comradery and prestige of being in the NFL, he decided that the likelihood of signing with a new team and being injured yet again was not something he relished. "Being part of a football team from the age of eighteen to thirty you realize that you need everyone's best efforts to achieve any goals; that everyone has a significant role and you are only as strong as the weakest link. It is never about you but the team," Deitan explained.

Deitan believes one of the attractions to police work is the relationship built between a law enforcement band of brothers and sisters. "We are all from divergent backgrounds, interests, religions, creeds, and we all come together for a common goal. Failure is never an option and quitting is not a part of our vocabulary. When you retire from football, it can leave a huge void, and that is why so many football players get depressed and find it hard to move on," Deitan explained.

"But joining the police department makes you feel like you belong to a new team. The selfless oath that you take to give your life to save a stranger is never about you. You have to be accountable, dependable, and strong," Deitan said. "I loved teamwork, solving problems, and helping people. All qualities that we learned on the gridiron—the adrenaline rush, quick decision-making, and adapting to unexpected things such as injuries, setbacks, promotions, and demanding work. A band of brothers and sisters that have each other's backs no matter what. I believe that becoming a police officer is a calling."

During this time of great excitement in Deitan's life, a tragedy occurred that affected him in ways he could not have anticipated.

"My older brother, Richer Dubuc, who was a constable for the Royal Canadian Mounted Police, had a lengthy career ahead and a wonderful family; then the unthinkable happened," Deitan said.

On March 6, 2017, when he was just forty-two years old, Richer was involved in a horrific vehicle accident. He died instantaneously and left behind a grieving wife and four children.

"The event was very traumatic and changed me in many ways. It made me appreciate the precious present even more because tomorrow is not a guarantee," Deitan reflected.

Deitan said his brother's partner had radioed that they were dealing with a dozen undocumented immigrants crossing the United States into Canada. Richer jumped in his unmarked SUV and headed down to the border from his station, which is a half-hour drive. He was on a two-lane highway when he passed a woman going seventy miles an hour. It was stormy and almost dark so visibility was reduced. Unbeknownst to him, there was a farm tractor going twenty miles an hour ahead of him without lights. "The impact was so intense that my brother severed his aorta and bled out before anyone could get to him. His vehicle black box showed he never even let the gas pedal go, indicating he must have been distracted for a moment and never saw the tractor in front of him. It was one of the worst days of my life," Deitan recalled.

But Deitan had to pull himself together, despite his tragic loss, and utilize his can-do attitude to learn how to become an effective and impactful police officer.

Deitan clearly loved to learn and experience every phase of police work he could. At the Minneapolis Police Department, he worked with the Rifle Team, Bicycle Rapid Response Team (BRRT), and Disaster Strike Team. He also became a SWAT negotiator. Always looking to improve his skills, Deitan asked to be transferred to North Minneapolis in 2012. That part of the city is considered the toughest—where gangs are prevalent, as well as drugs and crime overall. Deitan had his share of close calls, such as the time he was sitting in his squad car waiting for a tow truck to arrive. "A gang member fired at my car nine times. The shots went around my head, my leg, and my body, and I was lucky to be alive. Angels were on my shoulders that day because those rounds narrowly missed hitting me," Deitan recalled.

But there were many positive experiences as well.

Deitan worked with a host of caring and helpful mentors. "I always loved to learn from the men and women who came before me and were willing to help a young officer," said Deitan. After working for two and a half years in North Minneapolis, Deitan applied and was selected to be part of the Violent Criminal Apprehension Team (VCAT) where he would track down the most violent offenders throughout the metropolitan area. In that role, Deitan was on call twenty-four/seven and dealt with the worst of humanity. "These criminals are so callous and reckless, and they have no regard for life. No remorse. They are the rapists and murderers, and to deal with them day in and day out you have to develop a thick skin. The only thing that changes about these offenders for me is their name and where I apprehended them," Deitan explained.

After four and a half years as a member of VCAT, Deitan was promoted to sergeant, which required him to have an additional four months of training. As always, he was up for the new challenge. After the training, which included investigations with the Crime Against Children Unit and working in South Minneapolis as a street supervisor, Deitan was permanently assigned as a beat supervisor in South Minneapolis, where he worked for a year and a half building relationships with business owners and neighborhood associations. Then he was transferred to the Procedural Justice Unit as its head trainer. "The goal of that unit was to help other officers learn about historical trauma that African Americans experience as well as other disenfranchised groups such as Native Americans, Hispanics, and LGBTQ people," Deitan explained.

"The ultimate goal of procedural justice training with our police officers was to raise awareness of their own implicit bias and the effect that explicit bias can have in policing," Deitan said. "The vast majority of our officers were already well rounded, and this class was designed to reinforce what they already knew. I believed in what I was teaching, and I knew that it would have a positive impact on the future of law enforcement," he added.

(During that time, Deitan also received his master's degree in leadership from St. Thomas University; lifelong learning continued to be his passion. He also became a father to a daughter named Camille in 2006 and a son, Dylan, in 2007.)

After two years in the Procedural Justice Unit, Deitan had a conversation with one of his deputy chiefs and was offered a job to take over the Community Engagement Team—which works with the worst hard-hit violent crime neighborhoods in Minneapolis. He created the Gun Violence Reduction Initiative in collaboration with several neighborhood associations and numerous city stakeholders.

The main contributors were presidents of the two hardest-hit and crime-plagued neighborhoods in North Minneapolis—Diana Hawkins and Kathy Spann. "We had dedicated team members like Diana and Kathy, and together we created a program that was community based and community led. It did not rely on federal dollars but rather on the amazing work of those dedicated community leaders," Deitan added.

Then the murder of George Floyd happened. And the world of law enforcement changed forever.

Deitan's Gun Violence Reduction Initiative was shut down and the Minneapolis Police Department lost hundreds of officers. The Community Engagement Team was disbanded—due to the massive loss of officers and supervisors—and Deitan was transferred to a street supervisor position.

"Like most people, when I saw the video my heart sank," Deitan lamented. "I knew that the Minneapolis Police Department would never be the same. The riots that followed put a great stress on the police department and widened the rift between us and the community. I spent most of my career in law enforcement working so hard to build trust in neighborhoods that now lost trust in us. Minneapolis has so many amazing officers doing amazing work daily, and even though there are many stormy days ahead, I honestly believe things will get better," Deitan said.

Soon after George Floyd, there were calls across the country to "defund the police," and once again, police officers became the number one enemy. "This was a tough time for all of us good cops. We felt abandoned, unsupported, and unwanted," Deitan said.

Deitan said that the growing sentiment to defund the police had the unintended consequence of making the Minneapolis community and the city more unsafe. "Crime was up, carjackings increased, and 911 calls took longer to respond. I felt terrible for the community members because we worked so hard to build trust and maintain great relationships and now, I felt that it was eroding at an alarming rate," said Deitan.

"When you wear your uniform, you take an oath to serve and protect. I will do that every day and wear it proudly no matter what position I hold. While it is sometimes difficult to deal with on an everyday basis, we need to understand that people in the community are not mad at us personally, but the uniform and what it has represented for so many years," Deitan explained. "The mere presence of the uniform brings back over one hundred years of emotions," he added.

What can be done to rebuild trust between the minority community and the police? Deitan believes it is a simple fix. "No wheel has to be reinvented, and we cannot worry what else is going on the world. We have to focus on one neighborhood at a time. We have to start seeing what we have in our city and be open and honest in everything we do as police officers," said Deitan.

"Every initiative that the police department builds and creates with the community members has to be community led and community based. The police department does not need to be in the driver's seat, but a passenger that is part of the solution. Our safety and security has to come from within and we cannot rely on anyone else to save us. It is not about the money but the commitment of us all," Deitan said.

"We must go back to working on our community engagement as soon as possible because it has never been as crucial as it is now. Because of the cutbacks and the 'defund the police' attitude, so many relationships that took years to build were broken. This allowed mistrust to grow and that divides us even more from the people we serve. It is crucial that we return to our emphasis on outreach and community engagement. I am hopeful that we can go back to the amazing work we were doing prior to George Floyd," Deitan said.

What does the future hold for Deitan Dubuc? "Despite the challenges we all face in law enforcement today, I remain optimistic about the future. As the great Dallas Cowboys Coach Tom Landry once said, 'A champion is simply someone who did not give up when they wanted to.' I am hoping I can live up to his words."

Four

CANINE CONNECTION

The dog is a gentleman; I hope to go to his heaven, not man's.
　　　　　　　　　　　　　　　　　　　　　　　　—Mark Twain

A S A YOUNG BOY GROWING UP IN NORTH MINNEAPOLIS, MINNESOTA, Donnell Crayton learned how to protect himself from the eventual scourge of gunfire. His mother would instruct her five boys to duck under a table or lay down on the floor if they heard any "pop, pop, pop" sounds. His pet dog at the time ran into the other room and hid in fear. Thirty years later, Canine Officer Donnell Crayton is still living in Minneapolis, but this time arresting bad guys alongside his eighty-pound German Shepard and loyal best friend, Jett.

But Donnell's path toward becoming a full-fledged Minneapolis canine officer was a circuitous one, though it was clear even as a teenager that he had the chops.

As the middle child—with two younger brothers and two older ones—the conventional wisdom was that Donnell would be conflicted, misunderstood, and not as likely to succeed. Current research defies those stereotypes and, in fact, finds that middle children are more likely than their siblings to succeed, and they tend to be more independent, empathetic, and creative. That was certainly the case with Donnell.

But where he grew up would present immense challenges that even the most well-adjusted young black man would have to overcome. "We lived in a primarily black neighborhood, and we were surrounded by crime; mostly gang violence," Donnell said. "It was routine for us to fall to the floor as soon as we heard gunshots. And they happened all the time."

When Donnell was twelve years old, he was emotionally traumatized by the murder of another twelve-year-old, Tyesha Edwards. A gang member, Myron Burrell, who was sixteen at the time, was shooting at another gang member, and a stray bullet struck Tyesha as she sat at her dining room table doing her homework in South Minneapolis. This was in 2002. The shooter was convicted of first-degree murder, but the first trial was postponed because the Court ruled that the statement he made to the police was inadmissible. He eventually was convicted and sent to prison.

"Tyesha's senseless murder affected me terribly because she was around my age, and that could have been me sitting at our house getting shot," Donnell lamented. "Looking back, it might have been the first time I realized that I could do something to make sure this would not happen to any other kid."

Donnell never knew his biological father. He died before Donnell was born, but he never learned that his death resulted from drugs until he was a teenager. His mother wanted to protect Donnell and did the best she could to be both mother and father to her boys. "I was about nineteen or twenty before I asked about my dad. When my mom told me about his drug addiction, it really did not phase me; I just went about my day. You cannot feel for someone you never knew," said Donnell.

Donnell's mother remarried and was divorced after she and her sons had enough of her husband's violent outbursts. Donnell's stepfather was physically and verbally abusive and would punch and kick his mother on a routine basis. He had no concern that his stepsons heard the beatings or were in close proximity to the incidents. "When we were kids, we would hide in the room and it was devastating to me and my brothers," Donnell explained. "But as we grew up, five of us were no match for this creep. One day my brothers and I took a baseball bat, held it to his face, and wacked him right on his head. We kicked his ass and the next thing we knew he split."

Soon thereafter his mother got a divorce. "Times were tough, and we had to move to a homeless shelter where we all slept in one room," Donnell recalled. "But the irony was that it was certainly better than the violent relationship we all had to endure. It also has made me more sensitive to homeless people and the need to treat them with respect and dignity."

Though crime continued to plague the neighborhood, it was only committed by a small percentage of the residents. As Donnell explained, "they make hell for everyone else." Luckily, Donnell and his brothers were spared any of the bloodshed or participation in gang life. In fact, they thrived.

When Donnell was fourteen years old, he was hired at the Minneapolis Park and Recreation Board working with kids. The organization was created in 1883 and covers more than 6,800 acres of the park system, which continually is rated the number one park system in the United States. "Almost everywhere you look there is a park in our city, and I loved tagging along with the park police and watching them do their jobs," Donnell said. "When I was in my senior year in high school, I was dead set on becoming a doctor since I was in advance placement in all my science classes, especially chemistry and biology."

Kids growing up in the inner-city were taught from an early age that talking to the police was something you should never do. "You did not talk to police; they were the enemy. That is what I was taught until I met Officer Rowland. Even though he was a white guy, he took an interest in me, and it was not that long until I realized they were only regular guys," Donnell said. Over the four years Donnell was volunteering at the Park Board and getting to know and like Officer Rowland, he was surprised one day when he received an intriguing offer from his new-found friend.

"Hey, Donnell, do you want to come with me on a ride-along?" he asked.

"Man, I do not know but I will ask my mom," Donnell told him.

"One more thing, Donnell, are you eighteen yet?" asked Officer Roland. Donnell had just turned eighteen a few weeks before.

After Donnell's mother agreed to let him go with Officer Roland on a ride-along, Donnell met him at their headquarters on a Saturday morning in May. "Man, I had the time of my life. We chased a stolen car, stopped and talked to people in the community, and checked out some drug paraphernalia we found in one of the parks. I asked him, 'Is this what you all do every day?' Man, I am signing up for this," said Donnell.

Donnell realized that his dream of being a doctor was overruled by the excitement he felt during that ride-along. He did not want to go to school for another twelve years to become a doctor and instead, decided to explore how to become a Community Services Officer with the Minneapolis Police Department. This was an entry level position in law enforcement with the goal of training the applicant to eventually become a police officer. The training consisted of rigorous physical fitness tasks, department policy and procedures, law enforcement best practices, squad car maintenance, and more. The tuition was free, and if the person succeeded, they would be promoted to a recruit at the police academy. "I was so excited that I was about to become a police officer," Donnell said.

In 2008, Donnell graduated at the top of his class and was hired by the Minneapolis Police Department. But his jubilation was shattered when the financial crisis occurred and the country was experiencing layoffs and companies were entering into default or bankruptcy. Just as quickly as his law enforcement career began, it was over. Donnell was laid off. Forty of his classmates now needed to regroup and rethink their careers in law enforcement with the Minneapolis Police Department.

Donnell decided to call his friend and mentor, Officer Rowland, to ask if the Park Police might have a park agent entry job available. "Officer Rowland, I just got laid off from the police department and was wondering if you have a job for me? Let me know and I will apply," Donnell asked him, hoping for the best.

"Donnell, I have known you since you were a kid, and you are a fine young man. Go talk to the chief now and I will tell him you are coming," said Officer Rowland.

Brad Johnson was the chief of the Park Police and he also heard about Donnell's work ethic and all-around magnetic personality. "Look, I heard about you since you were fourteen and I know you are a great kid. I understand you have had adversity in your life, but you overcame it and you are a good person. You are hired and you can start on Monday," Brad told Donnell. "Their loss is our gain."

At twenty years old, Donnell became a member of the Park Police, which was an unsworn job and considered pre–law enforcement. (The State of Minnesota requires two years in the criminal justice program where, at the end, the applicant receives an Associate Degree. One more year of training enables the person to attend the Police Academy.)

Park agents work in the field everyday writing citations for parking violations, retrieving drug paraphernalia, and patrolling the parks that were frequently used by drug dealers, drug addicts, gangs, and other criminals. They also write citations for people walking around naked, not having their dogs on leashes, and other non-violent offenses. "People think of parks as places where people are happily playing Frisbee, or eating a picnic lunch, but here in Minneapolis that is not the case in some of the parks," explained Donnell.

"Drug users occupy park bathrooms, and we had to learn who the offenders are and how to deescalate a situation if we come across one. As non-sworn police personnel, we do not carry a gun so I had to be more observant and identify what pre-attack indicators are. Then once they are calm, we pat them down, search them for weapons or drugs, then place them in hand cuffs. In intense situations we call in a sworn officer. They are the only ones who could have a gun in the Parks Department," Donnell explained.

In the two-and-a-half years on the job, Donnell learned how to manage many real-life situations from officers more experienced and willing to help him.

During this time, Donnell, now twenty-one, finished his course work and received his associate degree in science and law enforcement; he made his mother proud.

But, unfortunately, no one was hiring police officers when Donnell graduated in 2010. He recalls that for every one thousand applicants, there were only one or two jobs available. So, Donnell continued to work for the Park Police, and after two years he began to wonder if law enforcement was the right choice. To supplement his income, a friend he knew from high school suggested he apply for a job as a special education assistant. In that role, he would help teachers with students in kindergarten through eighth grade who had mental health issues. This was right up Donnell's alley, given his experience working in law enforcement. "There was one time that two kids got in fight, and one threatened to kill himself and his fellow students. Eventually, he was taken to the hospital for treatment and evaluation. I realized he was serious, and he really did plan to kill other students. Eventually we found that he had hidden a knife in the bushes. This experience helped me deal with people with mental health issues since they respond better in a less confrontational manner," said Donnell.

Then, to his surprise, in 2012 Donnell got a call back from the City of Minneapolis to return to the Police Department. The budget was reinstated, and they needed community service officers. "I jumped on it," Donnell said. "Of the forty of us that were laid off, they only brought thirteen back. I had to return to the Academy, and in 2013 I graduated and was the first police officer in my family. It broke my heart that only one year later my mom died of Scleroderma, a disease of the autoimmune system. And she was only forty-four," Donnell recalled.

Donnell dealt with the loss by working hard to become a Minneapolis police officer of distinction, meaning he would learn as much as he could and perform at his personal best. His law enforcement skills would soon be put to the test in a series of high stress situations, many of which could have been deadly.

Among Donnell's first law enforcement experiences was a hostage situation where he was dispatched because of shots fired. When he arrived on the scene, his mind was racing. The shots were coming from a large apartment building on one of the upper floors. As he and his partner entered the building, they could smell gun smoke. On the police radio Donnell learned that the suspect had a hostage. Then they heard more gun shots in the hallway.

Since he was still in training, Donnell worked with more senior officers and the other law enforcement officers on the scene. "One of the hostages was released by the suspect. He was injured, and the paramedics were there to transport him to the hospital. I decided to jump in the ambulance with him, thinking I could get some intelligence as to whom the shooter was and what was going on that we could not see," Donnell said.

In the meantime, hostage negotiators were trying to communicate with the shooter, to no avail. "I was surprised that the victim gave me the full story, and it turned out he had an affair with the woman whose husband came home and found her with another man. The husband shot him in the hallway, then grabbed his wife, took her hostage, and dragged her into a neighbor's apartment," said Donnell.

After eight hours, the shooter released the hostage, and the decision was made to send in a robot in with a camera. It turned out that the shooter had turned the gun on himself and was pronounced dead. "The guy had killed himself. It happened so fast," Donnell recalled. "You have to figure it out on the fly. It was actually scary but at the same time I was excited knowing I would be doing this all the time. I also learned I have to be prepared and assume all calls could be serious and, at times, fatal. So, I tried to always have a plan, and if necessary, re-think my tactics in a split second."

Donnell said that new police officers do have constant field training with experienced officers that they can talk to about law enforcement best practices. "Having experienced guys available for you is essential. I could ask them, 'Hey, should I have done it this way? What do I need to do to improve?' They are there to teach you the ropes and grade you," Donnell explained.

There would be three more months of field training, firearms defensive critical incident training, learning how to deal with people with mental health issues, and the use of force. In the summer of 2013, Donnell finished his training and was assigned to a precinct and placed on the day shift. Eventually, he would also work the night shift when many of the homicides took place.

"Growing up in the city we had many shooting victims, but I never saw a dead body until that first experience in the apartment building. Even though some of the victims are bad guys, I still feel for them and their families. Even a bad guy is a human being and should not have died the way he did," Donnell explained.

For Donnell, as many of his fellow police officers will attest, emotions are hard to contain, especially when they arrive on the scene and the victims are children or grieving family members. "It was hard for me to find the right words to say as an officer, especially when I am on the perimeter and the family of the victim arrives. While it is part of our job to process the crime scene, it is equally important to console the loved ones until the chaplain arrives," Donnell explained. "In the meantime, I let them cry on my shoulder and tell them that I am sorry for their loss. That is where people lose sight of who we are as police officers. We are not knuckleheads only interested in bruising and arresting a bad guy. We are there at your worst moments, holding your hands. We are taught in the Police Academy not to be emotional and not let people see you sweat or in pain, but that is not always possible," Donnell said.

Donnell said he can generally leave work behind when he arrives home—but not always.

"When kids die by violence, that really affects you. Or when kids are hurt. They have no reason to be hurt. These situations eat at you, no matter how hard you try to suppress your feelings," said Donnell.

Donnell's next career move, before he would be assigned to the prestigious Canine Unit, was in 2015, when the gang unit opened up. At the time, in North Minneapolis, gang shootings were almost a daily occurrence and presented numerous challenges for law enforcement officers.

They needed to create an Intel Unit to centralize information and help law enforcement learn who the evolving hierarchy of gang members were and where they lived. "I was intrigued by the job and so I applied. I doubted I would get the job but somehow I did," Donnell recalled. "There were five officers and one sergeant assigned to the unit. I started working with the Intel Unit to identify and track and gang members. To find out who is who and what is what. It felt good to get guns off the street. I believe in the first year we got twenty-five guns off the street and engaged many new informants."

Interestingly, Donnell said social media is one of the best ways to track gang members. Why? "Gang members are narcissistic and like to show off and want everyone to look at them. They love to show off their fancy clothes, cars, money, and guns. Once you can identify them, you learn who is violent and focus on them," Donnell explained.

During the time Donnell was in the Intel Unit it expanded from five to fifteen officers and one hundred guns were taken off the streets every year. His unit also expanded partnerships with other agencies as well. It was so successful that Donnell and his colleagues would be asked to train officers throughout the state, sharing their tactics of talking to gang members and getting to know who they are and ways to keep their violent acts at bay.

But the hallmark of Donnell's career was about to commence. It would be a lifelong passion and intractable relationship with eighty-pound, majestic, fierce, and obedient German-born German Shepard, Jett.

Dark as night with shiny, almost glistening fur and intense intelligent eyes, Jett became Donnell's constant canine companion in crime fighting as well as his very best friend. "I was always interested in the Canine Unit. It was a highly coveted position normally based on seniority. I had no intention of leaving the [Intel] Unit but when I saw an email for the job, I decided to throw my name in the hat and apply," Donnell recalled. Donnell was the top candidate and, to his surprise, got the job in 2018, the same year he married his fiancée, Kendal. "I was sad to leave the [Intel] Unit but I always wanted to do something with dogs and this was my chance," he said.

Soon, Donnell was formally introduced to Jett, who was only eleven months old and an empty slate, but ready and willing to learn. Jett, as most dogs chosen for the Canine Unit, cost $10,000 and hailed from Germany from a long bloodline of German Shepards that became police dogs.

The bond was instantaneous, and Donnell knew he had found a job he would want for life. At the Canine Academy, Jett and Donnell would work together on Jett's training intensively for four months. Things such as obedience, criminal apprehension, evidence searching, recovering evidence, and learning to track a human scent. Then there was agility, where Jett would learn to jump over a six-foot fence or crawl under small spaces, for example.

The goal was for Jett to be certified to work as a police dog by the United States Police Canine Association.

Jett passed with distinction, and his potential for working in the Canine Unit of the Minneapolis Police Department was solidified.

Training dogs such as Jett is the hardest training program in the department, according to Donnell. "You have a sixty- or ninety-pound dog pulling you and you initially have to fight with them to make them do what you want them to do. But they learn through repetition, and in Jett's case, he is a quick study, especially when there are treats as rewards," said Donnell.

Jett, now four years old, has proven himself to be a professional canine crime fighter and loyal companion. He is also well-mannered and sweet, even letting Donnell's two-year-old yell at him and pet him—sometimes a little too rough. But do not let this handsome dog deceive. When he is on the job, he is confident and unafraid.

"Jett in the field is as good of a partner as I could ever have, regardless of the fact that I cannot ask him questions or have him answer me back," said Donnell.

Donnell recalled one time when Jett showed his tough dog training. There was a man that hijacked someone's car and took off with officers in pursuit. Donnell was the only canine officer on the scene at the time. The man crashed the car, ran out of the vehicle, and hid. "Jett knew which way he went and began to track his scent. He tracked the man for two blocks, then Jett pulled me into a bush on the side of someone's house. I made our standard canine announcement: 'I am with the canine police, come out or you will be bit.' Normally a suspect will obey your command and come right out of hiding, since they do not want to be bitten by a ferocious dog like Jett. But this time nothing happened. The next thing I knew Jett dove into the bushes and got something. It turns out it was the suspect," Donnell said.

Jett put his mouth around the man's thigh and pulled him toward Donnell. He was handcuffed and taken to jail.

"Jett's training came all together. It was eye opening and the most meaningful experience with Jett that is seared in my mind to this day," Donnell remembered.

Then, in 2019, there was a shooting at 3:00 a.m. in North Minneapolis, where shots were fired inside of a house, and officers learned the father was shooting at his family. The police set up a perimeter and told the suspect inside to come out. It was a chaotic scene. Jett and Donnell were in front of the house. The suspect finally came out of the house with his hands up. He laid on the ground and Donnell and the other officers thought they could cuff him, but he had other plans.

He stood up, turned around, and ran back in the house. "The negotiators tried to talk him into coming out again and said they would put the dog away if he did. Instead, rather than coming out peacefully, they heard shots that were fired by the man now brandishing a rifle.

"We had fifteen cops on scene. We heard and saw the rifle so we shot back. I had Jett in one hand and with the other hand I was shooting at the suspect. He goes down but then sits back up and starts shooting again. We returned fire. Then all the gunshots stopped," Donnell recalled. "We thought, *is he going to get back up?* I sent Jett in first and he pulled the suspect out of the house so officers would not have to enter the home to render aid and risk their own safety. Unfortunately, the suspect passed away. Despite the fact that he may have killed his entire family, there was a part of me that still felt sad that he died. He was still someone's family member," Donnell lamented.

Jett is just like one of Donnell's children. "We are close at home and on the job and when he is not in kennel, he will lay down by the door until I come downstairs," Donnell said. "He is my best friend, and I spend more time with him than my family. I can pick up Jett's dog cues and he knows my commands. When he is working, nothing can deter him from fulfilling his police duties. When we are at home, he is just one big ball of love."

Jett will work alongside Donnell until he is retired, around eight or nine years old. "We do not want them to have hip issues. We want our dogs to retire and live a decent life. Plus, police dogs are so highly trained that boarding kennels will not accept them because of liability issues. So, when we go on vacation, I can take Jett to the Canine Unit and they will gladly dog sit for me," Donnell added.

For the past decade-plus in law enforcement, Donnell has seen the best and the worst of human nature. He entered law enforcement to make a positive change in someone's life.

But he is dismayed that a few bad cops and politics give police officers like him and many of his colleagues a bad reputation. "We feel the same way about bad cops as anyone does, but it is disheartening when the public lumps us all into one negative category," said Donnell.

"I might make the right decision to use force, but if someone took a video and showed it to thousands of people, that force might appear excessive. The truth is that no force looks good. As a result, we become more hesitant in responding to things and we suffer from racial slurs, hate speech, and people treating us like we are the enemy. Believe me, that hurts," Donnell said.

Donnell added that after the 2020 killing of George Floyd that sparked world-wide protests—many resulting in looting and destruction—half of his department quit. He was equally outraged and realized the officer who put his knee on George Floyd's neck was wrong; he was one of the bad cops. Everyone knew. But because of all of the anti-police backlash, some of his fellow officers suffered from post-traumatic stress and other illnesses and felt as if their life's work had no meaning or purpose.

Despite the recent challenges of policing in America, Donnell still works every day to be part of the solution.

"The solution has to come from a loud and boisterous call for change from the community. They have to be behind it because crime is out of control, and they need us. I hope to let them know that we are there for them and we work hard every day to improve our policing practices. And I hope that the general public would see who we really are [and] why we choose to serve. I am still that bright-eyed, bushy-tailed kid inside. And I will always be there to stop a bad guy or console a family who lost a loved one to violence. Somebody must be there to help search for bad guys, and if we all leave, there will no one to stop them. I am sure Jett would agree that we can pray for a better day," Donnell concluded.

Five

A Sheriff for the People

We all have a role in keeping our communities safe. We also owe a measure of gratitude to the men and women in law enforcement who dedicate their lives on a daily basis to protect us.
— Cindy Hyde-Smith, United States senator from Mississippi

THERE IS A NEW SHERIFF IN TOWN. WHILE THIS PHRASE MAY EVOKE THE cinematic image of a Clint Eastwood movie—with the super tough sheriff riding into town on his horse—for Worcester County, Maryland's new sheriff, an old Ford pickup truck and a dream will do.

Meet Matt Crisafulli, a strapping, South Jersey–born law enforcement officer who has spent his entire career working in the service of others. From losing his father—a Vietnam veteran with severe PTSD—when he was barely five years old, to becoming the youngest sheriff in Worcester County history, Matt has turned his despair into becoming a crime fighter with heart. In the process, he has transformed the Worcester County Sheriff's Office into a national model for the best law enforcement has to offer.

Matt was born in 1974 in Stratford, New Jersey, a small town just fifteen miles from the birthplace of America, Philadelphia, Pennsylvania. His mother, Susan, always told Matt that he was his father's "little sidekick," following him around like a puppy everywhere he went. "My dad was my hero, even at such an early age," Matt recalled. "I always wanted to go with him to the parking garage he managed in Atlantic City. While I have very few memories of my dad, I do vividly recall holding his hand on the boardwalk and driving down the boulevard marveling at all the bright lights as we drove by."

His father, also named Matthew, enlisted in the US Army at nineteen years old. Unlike many young men at the time who were protesting the Vietnam War, Matthew felt the desire to serve. He also wanted to escape from his troubled childhood and periodic bouts with depression.

Matt's father was deployed to Vietnam in 1969, and it was there that he met his lifelong friend, battle buddy, and soulmate, Michael Williams. The two men never discussed what happened in the rice paddies of Vietnam with anyone, but Matt knew it must have been gut-wrenching. Michael—who everyone called, "Willie"—and Matt's father shared a common trauma that later would haunt both father and son for years.

Matt's father was in the US Army's 101st Airborne and was deployed to Saigon, South Vietnam (renamed in 1969 Ho Chi Minh City), which is where he and Michael Williams first met. Willie was a young black man from Harlem, New York and despite their diverse backgrounds, Matthew and Willie became remarkably close. They were inseparable, in fact, and soon discovered they had similar interests. Both men loved Motown music, especially Marvin Gaye, and bonded listening to the Temptations, Four Tops, and any other artists they could get their hands on. These young warfighters were deployed to a foreign and hostile land. They were able to acclimate and survive through music, their military training, and budding friendship. "My mom told me a touching story when I was young. She said that my dad and Willie were such good friends that my dad told Willie in no uncertain terms, 'Willie, if I ever have a son, I want you to be his godfather.' He agreed on the spot," said Matt.

Matt had no idea how that relationship between two young men serving their country in an unpopular war would someday change his life.

When the two battle buddies returned from Vietnam, Willie and his new wife, Joanne, made the decision to move from their home in New York City to New Jersey so the two friends could spend more time together. But the good times, and deepening friendship between Willie and Matthew, would tragically and abruptly end, leaving Matt with unanswered questions and years of anguish.

"I do not recall the day that completely turned my life upside down, but over the years I was able to finally piece things together," Matt said. This is what he recalls.

"When I was three years old, there was one day when my dad never returned home from his job in Atlantic City. I soon learned that it was not because of an issue at work, but because he was involved in a fatal car accident. My mom told me at the time that he fell asleep at the wheel of his car, drove across the median strip, hit a pole, and died instantly. It is hard to describe the feeling of grief and pain I felt learning that the man I idolized was suddenly gone. My mom would come into my room at night, sit on my bed, and try to comfort me, but as a young boy, I simply could not comprehend," Matt explained.

Matt said that when Willie heard about the accident, he and Joanne rushed over to their house. "I can remember Willie hugging me and feeling like I was all alone in the world," Matt said. "I guess I was."

"As I grew older, I was haunted by losing my dad so suddenly and dramatically, and because I was an inquisitive soul, I would ask questions but was never completely satisfied," said Matt.

Life was about to take another detour when Matt enrolled in college in 1994 and became a criminal justice major. Matt soon realized that police records are permanent, and he decided to call the Washington Township, New Jersey Police Department to finally get some definitive answers as to what really happened to his father that fateful day.

"For most of my life, my mom told me Dad fell asleep while driving home from work; she was only trying to protect me from finding out the truth. But when I was able to get the records from the police department, I was stunned. They revealed that Dad was a methamphetamine addict. It turned out it was a single vehicle crash, and when my dad's car hit the curb, it went airborne, then crashed into a phone pole and then a guard rail. Dad fractured his skull and was dead at the age of twenty-eight. I was relieved to finally know the truth, but it opened up an assortment of problems that haunted me for years," Matt explained.

Matt said that even forty-three years later he occasionally has dreams about the unexpected loss of his dad. The dream has Matt chasing after his father as the two are running through the woods. But Matt never catches him. "Everybody deals with death differently, but despite what happened I know how much he loved me and my sister. As a parent myself, I look at my two daughters and realize how much love my dad had for me," Matt said.

Over the years, Willie became the father that Matt wished he could have had. "Uncle Willie and Aunt Joanne were there for me and my family, and I know how devastated they were to learn the news. Even though Uncle

Willie never talked about the details of Vietnam, he did tell me that he loved my dad like a brother. One day he opened up and said something that to this day makes me smile. 'I am glad I met your pops. Boy, we were so close, and oh the stuff we did. We had a blast.' Uncle Willie said that when he and my dad would leave each other for one reason or another, Dad would make a peace sign and Uncle Willie a fist. It was their secret code of brotherhood," Matt recalled.

Matt added that he and his Uncle Willie have been in lockstep for thirty-four years. "Willie was my father figure and helped mold me into the man I am today. We would often have heavy talks about growing up, being a good person, and looking out for your family. He would always tell me to keep my head on my shoulders and stay true to my goals. He was one of the most stable male influences in my life, and for that I am eternally grateful," Matt added.

With a solid start, despite a devastating tragedy, Matt graduated from North County High School in 1992 and enrolled in Anne Arundel Community College in Maryland where the family moved in 1980. He took general studies and law courses, and then spent two years studying criminal justice. "I think the experience with my dad, and my natural curiosity and sense of purpose, led me to wanting to pursue a career in law enforcement," said Matt. "I graduated with an associate degree in criminal justice and thought that by enrolling in the police academy I would be more marketable." Matt was accepted and, in May 1995, graduated with honors from the Anne Arundel Police Academy; he was on his way.

With stellar credentials and an indomitable spirit, Matt applied to both the Baltimore City Police Department and the Pocomoke Police Department. Pocomoke was the first to respond and so, in July 1995, Matt moved to the Eastern Shore of Maryland to begin his career in law enforcement.

As with all police academy graduates, Matt first became a patrol officer. He had a knack for communication and decided that he was going to become the most innovative patrol officer at the department. He was serious. "Apparently, I communicated well with people and knew that community policing was the way to keep crime in check. I initiated many crime watch areas throughout the city and formed bonds with as many citizens as I could—not just the wealthy and well-connected," Matt said.

Some of the innovations Matt put in place were increasing crime watch programs, adding more lighting in high crime areas, creating environmental designs to deter crime such as taking down shrubs, and making citizens more aware and encouraging them to become liaisons with the police. Matt was also taking part in drug arrests and solving numerous burglaries and violent crimes, among other law enforcement tasks. "I was firing on all cylinders," said Matt. "I was leading arrests, and always trying to do that with the utmost care and respect, even for the most hardened criminals."

Matt found over time that people who were arrested or suspected of a crime would open up to him, and he would be able to uncover the truth and sometimes even get a confession. "I would lock someone up and they would generally still respect me," he said. "There was an occasion where one of the guys I arrested and brought back to the station got to talking and confided in me that he could not read. I met with him a number of times after his arrest and helped him understand letters as well as tried to teach him to read. He had a tough time but it was worth the effort," Matt added. "Everyone needs a fair break in life and even those who commit crimes deserve a level of respect," he added.

In June 1999, Matt heard through the grapevine that the Worcester County Sheriff's Department was hiring someone to work as the Drug Abuse Resistance Education (D.A.R.E.) officer; his friends and colleagues thought he would be perfect for the job. He applied and was hired March 1999. "When I first heard about the job, it piqued my interest, and I was motivated by having the experience with a drug-addicted father."

By that time, Matt was married to his wife, Gwen; soon she was expecting their first child, Monica Marie, followed by another daughter, Natalie. Working as the D.A.R.E. officer, while still doing classic police work, Matt became well-known in the community, especially among junior and senior high school students, parents, and people from all walks of life. He would partner with teachers as well and create programs to help kids keep away from drugs and alcohol at a young enough age where it might have influence. "With a severe opioid crisis in America as well as the proliferation of drugs in general, you have to start educating kids and their parents when they are still young and impressionable," said Matt. "I am so touched when I see a student of mine graduate from high school without ever being involved in drugs and becoming a young adult with character and purpose. It was one of the highlights of my law enforcement career."

But Matt's father was never far from his heart. "My father was always in my heart through each and every lesson that I taught to our students. Things such as making good decisions and learning the things they need to avoid in life, especially drugs. Losing my dad at such an early age was channeled into an energy later in my life to assist other people. It was as if when I was teaching the kids about the dangers of substance abuse, my dad was essentially speaking to me as if he were by my side," said Matt.

After twenty years in the Sheriff's Office, and moving up the ranks to sergeant, Matt was encouraged to throw his hat in the ring and run for Worcester County sheriff. With no political experience, but an ardent desire to serve and protect citizens and keep crime at bay in the county, Matt registered as a Republican candidate for sheriff in 2018. With little money, almost no backing from the established Republicans in the county, and a small volunteer staff, Matt used his drive, communication skills, and love of the local residents he served to launch his campaign.

His campaign slogan was more of Matt's own world view: "People over politics." And he meant every word. After knocking on doors, hosting block parties, and attending church services, baseball games, and countless events, Matt's ship sailed in. Though he and his challenger had a tough fight, Matt won the election, narrowly beating his opponent by a mere 124 votes. On a cool day in November, there now was a new sheriff in town!

Matt hit the ground running, using his experience, course work, and proven police strategies to make his department a model for the region and the county at large. He was distressed by the negative attention in the news, especially when there were legitimate cases of police brutality. Not on his watch. "I started by sending my deputies to peer support training, then selected in-house trainers to form a team to meet with outside mental health services. I wanted to help our men and women cope with the stresses of the job, which I knew had to be addressed," said Matt. "They helped us learn what to look for as far as behavior changes, job performance changes, and bringing that awareness to our deputies really helped," said Matt.

"I also stood firm in my pledge to the citizens of Worcester County and did not engage in negative political banter. I reaffirmed what I planned to do for them and stayed true to that. Of course, I did make some mistakes. I wish I would have been more open-minded to the ideas that were initially presented to me by the former administration and the commanders I inherited. Thankfully, I realized that and was determined to get it right," Matt explained.

Matt said that when he first became sheriff it was as if he were on a roller-coaster that was constantly in motion. Things moved so quickly that at times he had to pivot, but he knew that was all part of being an effective leader. "Hindsight motivates you to be a thoughtful and initiative-taking leader and be able to recognize and reevaluate your office on a daily basis. You have to look in the mirror at your own mistakes to identify and correct them," Matt added.

As part of his new role, Matt instilled a culture that is mission-focused and citizen-centered. "Part of the mission of our agency is to provide exceptional services to our residents. Customer service is number one even if you cannot solve the problem; it is the way we treat our residents that counts," Matt said.

Aware of the climate in the country and the negative publicity regarding cases of police brutality, Matt said all citizen complaints are investigated thoroughly to determine if it is a training or discipline issue. Then the appropriate steps are taken as a solution. "I will not tolerate any misconduct or disrespectful behaviors from my men and women," Matt said. "Our deputies are also trained that even when force has to be used, they must show concern for the person's well-being and provide medical aid, if needed, immediately. It is our mission. No other behavior will be tolerated by me or my command staff."

With only three years on the job, Matt has made a variety of changes and is proud of his newly assembled team. "Forming a strong command team, getting deputies out of their cars, and having daily contact with residents helps solidify relationships and partnerships in our county. We are making positive changes in lives of people from all levels of society. We do not judge color; the law is color blind," said Matt.

Matt said his fellow sheriffs in Maryland have the same goals for their agencies. "We all realize and are proud of the fact that we were all elected for and by the people. There are no political parties. As a sheriff you fight for every person in your county," he added.

And like many of his peers in law enforcement today, Matt is disheartened when he hears a story of police brutality or incompetence. "No one hates bad police officers more than a good police officer. We are fighting this battle and we are under the microscope, as we should be," Matt said. "But it gives us an excellent opportunity to make sound decisions. Sometimes those decisions are not always understood. For example, there are times when force has to be used and yet the public may feel it was unnecessary. We follow the letter of the law and make sure any use of force is justified, and our deputies are acting appropriately," Matt said.

Matt believes that most police officers are caring, decent people, willing to risk their lives every day to serve and protect residents. He witnesses that kindness and compassion on a daily basis. "Just last week I got a call from a resident who lost a family member, and they said our deputy stayed at their home for hours to comfort them. Another time I received a letter from a resident who told me that one of our deputies saw them pulled over on the side of the road with a flat tire. The deputy helped change the flat tire and stayed with the resident until the tow truck arrived. It is the simple things like this that show that we still have phenomenal law enforcement officers and citizens appreciative of the men and women who put their lives on the line every day," Matt explained.

In July 2022, Matt won the Republican primary for Worcester County Sheriff, beating his opponent by more than four thousand votes. Since he has no Democrat opponent, he will return as Worcester County Sheriff for another four years. He knows he has had influence in enhancing the lives of the people he was sworn to serve and protect. "It is the honor of my lifetime to be the sheriff of Worcester County; I hope at the end of the day, people will know how much I care and appreciate all that they have given me. Most of all, I know my dad would be proud," Matt said.

PART TWO

EMTS AND PARAMEDICS TO THE RESCUE

Six

SAVING LIVES WITH KINDNESS

Next to creating a life, the finest thing a man can do is save one.
—Abraham Lincoln

IT WAS JUST ANOTHER DAY ON THE JOB FOR AMY ROYER. THAT WAS UNTIL she noticed a little boy walking with his mother and baby sister in front of her fire station. She dropped her gear and called out to the mother, "Excuse me, ma'am, would your son like to come in and take a look at our ambulance and fire truck?" The look on the boy's face was priceless. "Pure joy," Amy recalled. Together, they toured the fire station. Amy lifted the little boy about three feet so he could check out the inside of the ambulance; she even helped him turn on the emergency light bar. He was mesmerized. "He pointed to everything," Amy recalled. "It was like his mind could not keep up with his curiosity." However, the adventure was far from over. Amy asked his mother if he would like to see how the fire engine worked. She felt a wave of emotion envelop her as she watched the boy sit in the front of the fire truck, marveling at the massive hoses and numerous shiny instruments.

When the tour was over, the boy's mother thanked Amy repeatedly for the "amazing and unexpected adventure," and for inviting her son into a fire station for the first time in his young life. Amy hoped that the experience would be a positive memory for the child to remember someday.

Why did Amy decide to embark on this random act of kindness? She explains it this way: "A drug dealer would not think twice about handing a child drugs, so why not hand them something good and positive?"

65

This is how Amy Royer rolls.

Her interest in service began in a small, rural Bethlehem, Pennsylvania high school. When Amy was seventeen, she dated a first responder and was fascinated by the stories he told her. Things such as how he resuscitated a young man after a terrible car accident, stopped the bleeding after a gunshot wound, and consoled family members during the worst times in their lives. For a young and impressionable woman, these tales were intoxicating.

"I tried college for a brief time, but it was not for me, so I dropped out and focused on figuring out what I wanted to do with my life," Amy said. One Saturday in December, Amy and her friends headed to the mall; that trip changed her life.

As Amy walked toward one of her favorite boutiques, she noticed a promotional stand that was offering information on EMS services, including how to become an emergency medical technician (EMT) or a paramedic. EMTs differ from paramedics in that they are trained only to provide basic life support, including cardio-pulmonary resuscitation (CPR) and automated external defibrillator (AED) usage as well as other basic emergency actions. Paramedics receive advanced medical training and can perform intubations, cardiac monitoring, and administer medications, among others. They are the highest level of licensure of pre-hospital emergency care.

Rather than venturing into the boutique, instead Amy decided to check out the EMS booth. Initially, she was intrigued by the impressive-looking men in uniform staffing the booth. She imagined they were tough, and she was a bit intimidated. But she mustered up the courage to introduce herself to one of them, a six-foot-plus man with broad shoulders and an imposing demeanor. "Hi, my name is Amy Royer, and I am interested in learning how to get involved and possibly becoming an EMT," she said, having no clue how he would respond. *Would he think I was just a teenager with no actual intention of getting involved?* she wondered.

To her surprise, he was genial and took her request seriously. He was clearly impressed by her enthusiasm, but later mentioned to Amy that he wondered if she was just flirting or was serious about wanting to sign up.

"Well, Amy, how about stopping by the fire station tomorrow and we can talk? Then, if you think you want to see what we are all about, you can do a ride-along and find out if this line of work is for you." The man smiled a bit disingenuously. That all changed when Amy showed up at the fire station the next day, clearly ready to roll.

Amy was pumped. She thanked the man at the booth and left the mall determined to visit his fire station in the morning.

Sleep was elusive that night, but that was not an issue for Amy. She was beyond excited. She woke up way before 7:00 a.m., when she planned to head to the station. Little did she realize that her first ride-along would be harrowing and oddly exhilarating at the same time; it marked the beginning of a lifelong passion for helping others and saving lives.

That first ride-along proved to be a memorable one. "I felt like I was on steroids that day. Our first stop was a cardiac arrest, and then we had to be on scene for a car fire. Then, after the car fire we had yet another cardiac arrest. Wow, was this baptism by fire or what?" Amy recalled.

When Amy and the other EMS personnel returned to the station, Amy followed them outside the bay where the guys were smoking and talking. She thanked them for taking her with them on the ambulance and wondered what she should do next. As Amy was heading out of the station, one of the EMTs asked, "Hey, Amy, are you coming back tomorrow?"

Her hands were shaking. Her mind was racing. "Of course I am," she said, as she tried to appear composed and professional. Amy was motivated by the calm, compassionate care they had given to the victims that day. Even though Amy realized the job was fast-paced, requiring immediate actions, she welcomed the challenge if it meant making a difference in someone's life. As she left the station and headed home, she thought, *Yes! I have to do this.*

The next day proved to be the beginning of Amy's life-altering experience. She was greeted warmly by the guys in the station. The captain approached her, appearing welcoming as well. "Amy, you did a heck of a job today and all of the team were impressed with your enthusiasm. I would be happy to have you work here, and I would even sponsor and train you if you are interested." Those were the words Amy was longing to hear.

"Yes, sir, count me in," she said enthusiastically.

Amy was excited and at the same time shocked that she actually received a solid job offer. "I was only nineteen years old and living at home with my parents and brother in Bethlehem, Pennsylvania. Now I was about to become a real EMT. My parents were so happy for me and thrilled that I nailed the ride-along; I was on my way."

Amy could hardly wait to be part of the EMT team, even though she was still essentially an unpaid intern. During her first week on the job, she noticed that the guys were kind and respectable and had no problem answering all of her questions. And Amy asked a lot. "I asked them things such as, 'When you have cardiac arrests do you always have to have a driver and medic present? How do you do CPR in a moving ambulance? How do you determine how much percentage of a person's body was burnt in a fire, and how do you report that information to the hospital? Can you place an IV in parts of the body other than the arm?'"

The other EMTs and paramedics were clearly impressed with Amy's interest and enthusiasm. They signed her up on the spot for the EMT class. It is a six-month program with course work and hands-on skills training. Amy passed her tests and received her EMT certification in 1991. Before long she was volunteering on an ambulance and changing the course of her young life—saving others in the process.

When Amy began her career, she was only one of two women among thirty often "politically incorrect guys," Amy explained. "I guess you could say I was fresh meat. I was young, skinny, and pretty, and I did get a lot of attention. But I did not want attention in that way; I wanted to be part of the team," she said. One of the other EMTs asked Amy, during the first week after she received her certification "Are sure you can lift this person?" She was incredulous.

"I would not have taken this job if I could not do it," Amy replied.

"Okay, Amy," he said. "He's all yours."

It took a while for Amy to be accepted as "just one of the guys" until she was a few years older. However, Amy demonstrated her EMT chops after running as a volunteer for only six months. (One year after receiving her EMT certification, she became a paid official member of the EMS team.)

Amy had come a long way since that first ride-along where she had a tough time dealing with her first real-life emergency. In fact, after that car fire, Amy leaned over a bridge near the accident and threw up. That first whiff of burning flesh—which she describes as a person's hair burning but a "zillion times stronger"—is something that no one in the business ever forgets. "At first, I was physically sick from the smell of it, but you do start to get used to the ugly smells. But they are never emotionally easy to take," Amy said. "We used to put Vicks under our noses to mask some of the smells, but that did not work every time."

That would not be the last case where Amy had trouble coping.

One of the calls that affected Amy deeply and caused her to suffer from post-traumatic stress disorder (PTSD) was a house fire she had to attend.

A man and his two children were living in the house. The man had the gas burner on in the kitchen and then lit a cigarette. The blast lifted him in the air—eight feet, Amy recalled—and his body was violently blown out of the back door. The firefighters ran to his aid, pleading with him to let them know where his kids were located in the house. Tragically, when the firefighters entered the burning building, the children were not in the places the father thought; instinctively they knew the children would not survive.

The firefighters continued to search the house, as they struggled to breathe from the dense smoke. After moving from room to room, they finally located the lifeless children and brought them outside where the EMTs and paramedics were waiting. "It was such a horrible sight," Amy said. "I felt my heart sink in my chest and struggled to compose myself. I wanted to scream. But I knew we had to get to work and perform CPR even though we knew they were gone. The children died of smoke inhalation; there was nothing more we could do to save them," Amy recalled.

Amy and her team transported the children to the local emergency room, where they learned that their mother was working there as a nurse. It was heartbreaking. They had to remove her from the ER before her deceased children arrived. "It hit me hard and all of our team as well." Amy said. Most people do not realize that not only do the victims suffer, but the first responders as well. Fortunately, after major traumatic events, the department has a method for helping them cope with difficult calls like this. "A debriefing team was put in place and all of the stations that were affected were invited back to console one another and receive professional counseling," said Amy. "Some of us were crying, others were numb, but no matter what, these tragedies are harder to deal with when they involve kids."

Later in the day, the professionals designated to help arrived at the fire station. Amy and her team sat in a circle and a member of the clergy, a debriefing counselor, and EMS staff were there. They were part of the CISM (Critical Incident Stress Management) team and were brought in to help facilitate the group. "The first thing they ask you is what part you played in the call. Then they ask each of us how we are feeling and if we are having trouble dealing with the trauma. We have an open forum and are encouraged to talk about everything. Plus, they told us not to hesitate to call them day or night whenever we needed someone to talk to," Amy said.

She added that the crisis professionals look for signs of trauma such as not eating or sleeping, having nightmares, or not being able to focus on the daily aspects of the job. They also gave the group a list of warning signs of PTSD to watch out for. "This loss affected me to my core, and in fact, I called the counselors a few times as a result of my pain. In the beginning, every time I drove by in my car and saw a kid playing, I would always think to myself what I could have done better or was there anything I missed that could have saved their lives? But mostly I just cried. You learn to deal with stress—it can make or break you. I soon learned that the strong survive and how to work to build a tough skin. But no matter what, it was a bad, bad week for us," she added.

Amy and her team had their share of other tragedies that week, including a small plane crash where two people were burned to death. "We had a young, junior EMT on the call who was not certified and could only assist but not touch the victim. He was so devastated by the experience that all he could do was sit in the parking lot alone; he was in a daze. I asked him, 'What is going on?'"

Amy was aware of the terror he was feeling. His face was pale, and she noticed his hands trembling. "The young man told me he could not do the job, so I put my arm around him to try to stop him from crying. He said there was no way he could ever be an EMT. All I could do was try to comfort him," Amy recalled. "At that point he just needed someone to listen and give him the support he needed in dealing with such a tragedy."

Many years later Amy heard through the grapevine that the young man became a firefighter; she was touched.

Then there were those calls that Amy welcomed and did not involve drama. For example, Amy and her colleagues often respond to calls where a person falls and cannot get up from the floor. "This is where bedside manner comes in and it is among the most rewarding parts of the job.

"When person is in distress, they need a calm and steady voice to help them relax and feel secure. Sometimes I even joke with them if the situation calls for that. Most of the time I ask them lots of questions such as, 'How did you fall? Does anything hurt?' Many of those calls come from people living alone. We are their only lifeline and that is why it is so important to have a conversation with them and make them as comfortable as possible," Amy said.

Amy said there are those calls that require the EMTs to transport a nursing home patient to and from doctor's appointments. She recalls a man whose name was Tom—a bilateral amputee—who was in a county nursing home because his money ran out. "I would often see Tom sitting alone in his wheelchair in the hallway when we were making a call at the nursing

Lissette and her Harley Davidson *(Family photo)*

Lissette out of uniform and in style *(Family photo)*

Evan on duty

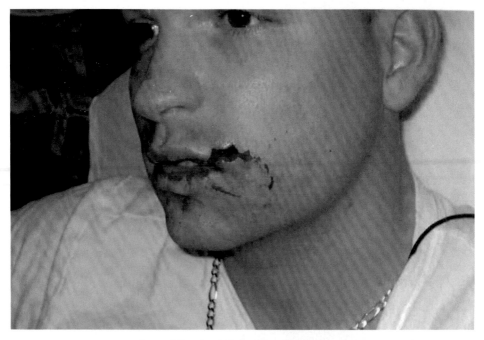

Evan following his dog bite *(Family photo)*

Deitan during his NFL career *(National Football League)*

From fanny pack to duty belt *(Family photo)*

Donnell enjoying a day at the beach *(Family photo)*

Donnell's K9 partner, Jett *(Family photo)*

Donnell and Deitan—the dynamic duo *(Family photo)*

Matt visiting his father's grave with his daughter, Monica-Marie *(Family photo)*

Matt's official photo as Sheriff of Worcester County *(Worcester County Sheriff Dept.)*

Amy striking a pose in her EMT uniform *(Family photo)*

Amy with her two sons—Jacob and Jimmy *(Family photo)*

Sarah in good spirits at work *(Family photo)*

Sarah and Padraic on the job (*Jaschell Walbert*)

Padraic, his mom Maggie, and sister Erin *(Family photo)*

Padraic at work *(Family photo)*

Kris working at Pocono Raceway *(Family photo)*

Kris in his Advanced Lifesaving Ambulance *(Family photo)*

David in his role as constable *(Family photo)*

David and his family of volunteer firefighters (left to right) Joey, David, Janet, and Mikey
(Family photo)

Woody, as Elvis, performs at his mother's nursing home *(Family photo)*

Woody in his dress firefighter uniform *(Family photo)*

Nicole takes a break after a tough day (*Shakesville.com*)

Nicole and her two sons—Justice and Walker (*Novato Fire*)

Jimmy relaxing on a day off *(Family photo)*

Jimmy and his wife and two daughters *(Family photo)*

Joey willing and ready to serve *(Family photo)*

US Marine recruiter, George, congratulates Joey on his enlistment *(Family photo)*

Dan on one of his numerous visits to Walter Reed *(Family photo)*

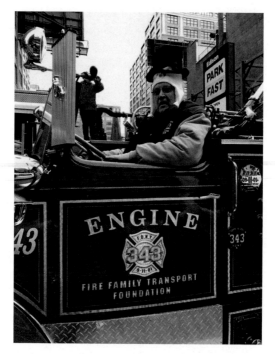

Dan drives Engine 343 to support the Fire Family Transport Foundation *(Family photo)*

home. I decided one day to talk to him. 'Hey, do you want to go down to the cafeteria and have a cup of hot chocolate?' I asked him. My partner had to do paperwork before leaving anyway so it gave me the perfect excuse. We had found a couple of seats in an empty room, and Tom really opened up. He told me about all the highlights of his life. It was extremely sweet," said Amy. Amy believes that people often tend to write off the elderly or those patients living in nursing homes; her job gives her the opportunity to change that paradigm.

During one Christmas visit to the nursing home, Amy was touched when Tom brought her a gift. "He was the sweetest man, and I looked forward to stopping by that nursing home as often as I could just to see him. I wish more people would visit the elderly; loneliness is among the saddest situation I have seen. Everyone deserves compassion and respect," she added.

In other situations, Amy said EMTs go on calls that actually make them happy. Delivering babies are among the highlights; she has had her share of those. There are even times when consoling a family member can be a meaningful experience. "There was this time that we got a call that a woman's husband was in cardiac arrest; it turns out he was dead for hours. Blood was pooling and rigor set in. We had to wait for the coroner and legally we cannot leave until the body is removed," Amy said. "Our job then becomes a mission to console the family. We are not necessarily trained to do that, but I do my best. Often times I just sit close to them and let them cry on my shoulder, if that is what they need. It makes you feel good, knowing you helped a family cope during the worst day of their lives," said Amy.

Then there is the crazy.

"We EMTs always expect the crazy. For example, people like to shove things inside their bodies, if you can believe, that obviously should not be there. Like the time a woman put a Coke bottle inside of an unmentionable location. She was fooling around with her boyfriend and the Coke bottle broke in pieces. That was quite an experience," Amy said. "It is amazing what people do to themselves. Sometimes we have to hold back a laugh, and we always wonder what the funk were they thinking?"

Amy decided to retire from her role as an EMT in 1993 to raise her young children. She was married at the time, but, unfortunately, the marriage did not last. She went back to work as an EMT in 1997, and soon met the love of her life on a Facebook dating site. His name was Kris Vierling—a paramedic—and the two became inseparable.

Now, she reflects on ten years on the job and hundreds of 911 response experiences.

"The best part of the job is getting to know the wonderful people you work with and their spouses. We do become an extended family, and there is nothing I would not do for them. I loved every minute," said Amy.

Amy never considered herself a hero. "I didn't want to be a hero; I just wanted to be someone's support; someone's ear; someone's voice. I loved helping people and held my head high. I was proud of what I did; I found my purpose," said Amy.

Her last day on the job was nothing short of hysterical—at least for the guys. Amy's fellow EMTs had a plan. And it included a traditional hazing—one last laugh.

Her fellow EMTs signed Amy up for her last shift before they left the station the night before. And true to form, a call came in from the dispatcher. No rest for the weary—even on an EMT's last day on the job.

Amy, the paramedic, and another EMT jumped in the ambulance to respond to the call. "They were messing with me," Amy said. "Minutes before we got in the ambulance, one of the guys shoved a hose in the back of my pants and turned it on. I was horrified! I insisted that I could not go on a call for a cardiac arrest with wet pants. What was I going to do? I realized I had no choice but to go on the call with sopping wet pants, and that is what I did," Amy recalled.

Amy was sitting in the back of the vehicle with her pants totally drenched. She knew she had to change them before the ambulance arrived on the scene. "I yelled to the driver and paramedic upfront that if either of them turned around and saw me naked I would never speak to them again. I watched them in the mirror until I was fully dressed to make sure they were not looking. I am happy to report they kept their word," she recalled.

"I am going to miss my first responder family," Amy added. "I am so proud knowing I helped many, many people. I kept them alive—at least until they got to the hospital—and comforted family members by helping them remain calm in a very tough situation," she added. "Most of all, I learned that all people—no matter their race, religion, or creed—all bleed red."

"Being an EMT is the most amazing job I could have ever had. You do it because you love it—and certainly not for the pay. Short of being in the military, it is the best job you can have in terms of serving your community," Amy said.

Amy encourages young people to consider EMS as a career. "If you want to know more about being an EMT, just stop by your local fire station and knock on the door. Or talk to a first responder when you see them at a football game, a concert, or any special event. You will not only save lives, but it might just save yours as well," Amy concluded.

Seven

Love in an Ambulance: Part One

One word frees us of all the weight and pain in life: That word is love.
—Sophocles

SARAH WALBERT WAS NOT SEARCHING FOR LOVE WHEN SHE DECIDED TO become an emergency medical technician. After three career changes, and a few personal ones as well, Sarah decided her dream job would involve helping others; she thought that becoming an EMT would fulfill that dream. Little did Sarah realize that her career choice would lead her to meeting the man she would eventually marry—he would be sitting right next to her in an ambulance.

Sarah, thirty-seven years old, was born in Allentown, Pennsylvania. She describes herself as a tomboy and a shy child, though she was always active in her church and local sports. Growing up as a Baptist, though she does not practice anymore, Sarah spent her childhood and teen years taking part in church activities. She attended church services every Wednesday evening and always on Sunday. "I was inspired as a child to be caring and reach out to help others," Sarah said. "When I attended the Gateway Christian School, my realization that volunteerism could be a way of life was reinforced. And since there were only twelve kids in my class, I was able to gain confidence and a sense of purpose."

The only disadvantage, Sarah pointed out, was that by being in such a small school she did not really interact with people outside of her small circle of friends. Luckily, she had a close relationship with the friends she did have, as well as her brother, Shane, who would later become her unwitting mentor.

During high school, Sarah began working at the Walker Technical Company, an organization that repairs pipe organs, not too far from her home. At the time, it was not a desired or typical profession for a young woman. Sarah couldn't care less. "I received a lot of experience with wiring on the pipe organs as part of my job. Most people do not realize that each button on the organ has more functions than just making one sound, so you really have to know what you are doing when you are fixing them," said Sarah. "The wire pipe organ is also partially electronic, which requires another set of skills. I have to thank my brother, who also worked there, for teaching me about making circuit boards and helping me learn this very technical skill," she added.

When Sarah was twenty, she left the Walker Technical Company. "Let me just say that I made some 'mistakes,' and in 2005 I became pregnant and a single mom. After I had my son, Derek, I needed to make more money to take care of him, so I took a job at Big Lots. But the position never paid me what I needed to raise my son, so I left," Sarah said. But as she would soon discover, her next adventure would thrust her into a field that would change her life in ways she never expected.

There was a local hospital—Lehigh Valley Hospital in Lehigh Valley, Pennsylvania—that Sarah noticed needed someone to work in a cleaning support capacity. She jumped at the chance to apply, though it was not a position that she coveted. But it did give her access to the healthcare environment and that was appealing to her. "When I was working in the hospital, I had a chance to witness so many interesting things and loved the fact that maybe someday I could be part of a team that would be hands-on with patients. It soon became obvious to me that cleaning was not my calling," she said.

She would soon discover that working in a hospital would not be either. "The floor I was working on at the time was a critical care floor; I noticed that the nurses would spend only about ten minutes on actual patient care and the rest of the time charting. At some point I knew that if I were to become a nurse, I would want to spend a lot more time with my patients," said Sarah. That realization ended Sarah's job at the hospital and her thoughts about ever becoming a nurse.

Sarah took a detour from working full-time and decided to attend college for photography. She continued to work part-time at the hospital, while taking classes an hour away from her home. "My friends and family thought I was all over the place, but I have always loved photography and had to see if I could make a go of it," Sarah said. "I realized that I could always return to the healthcare field if becoming a photographer did not pan out."

Sarah was accepted to the Antonelli Institute and was an excellent student. She was at the top of her class and graduated alpha beta kappa in 2009 with a degree in photography. Before graduation, one of her final projects was to take photographs of "real-life" situations and document them with her camera. Since the hospital transferred Sarah to the Emergency Room, she decided that would be a good place to start. After explaining the project to her bosses, they agreed to give Sarah access to the patients, if she agreed not to reveal their identity and comply with HIPPA privacy laws.

"I must have taken hundreds of photos of ambulances coming into the ER. I was mesmerized by what they did to help the patients. It was fascinating," Sarah said. Soon she would get to know the EMTs and paramedics by name and had an idea for her photography project. "I asked one of the guys I knew fairly well by that time if I could go on a ride-along in the MEDEVAC helicopter and in an ambulance to take my photos. I was incredibly surprised that he agreed," said Sarah.

Sarah's graphic photos of patients being taken to the hospital with severe injuries or other medical emergencies were so riveting that she received an A from her professor. While Sarah was thrilled with her grade and loved photography, soon the reality sunk in that making a living with a camera was not in the cards; she needed a steady income to take care of her special needs son.

"I had fun doing that until the end of school, when working part time in the ER and driving an hour each way to Philly for school was just too much. I needed a break and some time off; I was exhausted," she said.

Sarah finally decided to put photography on the back burner.

Sarah went back to the hospital full time. Her bosses noticed her drive and excellent interpersonal skills, so they decided to train her to become a technical partner. That meant that she could assist with direct patient care.

During that time, Sarah thought seriously about reconsidering her decision to become a nurse. Derek was four at the time. Everything was on track and going well for Sarah until she injured her back lifting a patient from her bed to the wheelchair. As a result, she developed a herniated disc; her nerve pain was so severe that at times she could not even feel her feet. She had to take a leave from her job at the hospital to recover. Sarah's condition eventually improved with medication, surgery, therapy, and time; soon Sarah was ready to go back to work. But where?

"I did not want to go back to the hospital, so I sent in tons of applications to other jobs in healthcare but never heard back from any of them," Sarah said. "It was so depressing."

Then by chance, Sarah noticed an advertisement in the local paper that the Cetronia Ambulance Company in Allentown, Pennsylvania was hiring. She was ecstatic! "I put in an application on the spot and the head of human resources actually returned my call. I was pumped until the person on the phone said there was a hiring freeze and told me to get back to them after August. I desperately wanted the job, so there was no question that I was going to call them back," Sarah added.

During that trying waiting period, Sarah was determined to get the job. She concocted a plan to overcome any objections about her physical abilities to perform. Sarah went to the gym every day and even hired a personal trainer. She worked day and night to convince Cetronia she was ready and able to work. After calling back another time, only to hear the hiring freeze was still in place, Sarah decided to give it one more try. Luckily, the third time was the charm; she was hired!

In the beginning, Sarah just pushed wheelchairs around and drove nursing home patients to and from doctor's appointments. But those first days back in healthcare were exhilarating; Sarah was hooked. She found her true north. And soon she would meet the man of her dreams.

Sarah was never the type of person to sit at a desk, and her new employer recognized her suitability for a physical job as well. So much so that they honored her request for a scholarship to attend a six-month EMT course. The only stipulation was that she would work for the ambulance company for two years after graduation. That was a small price to pay for pursuing her newfound passion.

In her EMT class was a young man named Padraic, a fellow student who had the same goals as Sarah. She was mesmerized by his good looks and intelligence. As she got to know him, she found herself attracted to his kind nature and care for others. She felt extremely comfortable with him and one day had an unusual request.

"There was another guy hitting on me on the job and he kept sending me creepy text messages. So, I asked Padraic if he could say we were dating just to get this guy off of my back," she recalled. Padraic was "sneaky," Sarah said, when she proposed the unusual request. Padraic offered her an interesting counter proposition. He told her: "Sarah, you can say you are dating me but only on one condition—you go out on a date with me." He was sneaky, in Sarah's opinion, but it was an offer she could not refuse.

In March 2016, and with her relationship with Padraic blossoming, Sarah received notification that she passed the EMT certification exam; Padraic did, as well. Four days later, Sarah and an all-female crew went to work; Padraic would soon follow.

* * *

"As an EMT you never forget your first cardiac arrest," Sarah explained. "You don't always know what caused it. It could be drug-related, lack of oxygen to the brain, or cardiac issues. Even though we had multiple courses in CPR, muscle memory, defibrillation, and clearing an airway, nothing can prepare you for seeing a person in cardiac arrest for the first time; it can be extremely messy," Sarah explained.

Having a good partner is critical, according to Sarah. "We must always have each other's backs; anticipating every move. We need to work quickly in an emergency. Teamwork gets the job done effectively and efficiently and we need to think as one with four hands," Sarah said.

Sarah said she learned quickly not to look directly into a patient's eyes. "When someone is in a state of extreme distress, they appear lifeless, and their eyes are glazed and not tracking. Here you are trying to save a person's life and despite doing everything in your power that does not always happen. It can affect you for months."

But despite the emotional and physical challenges that being an EMT entails, Sarah was thrilled to be part of a profession that has deep roots in empathy and love. "I was happy that I was able to help people and comfort them as they struggled to survive. Before, I could only transport a patient. Now I actually help save them; it is a dream come true for me," Sarah said.

Being an EMT is a grueling profession and the most dangerous among first responders. There are twelve-hour shifts where a person might care for two, four, or six patients during one shift alone—often not having a moment to take a breath, let alone eat or drink. "I remember one of my worst days with my BLS [basic lifesaving] crew where we did eleven transports. One trip was to a hospital in Philly, and we made two separate trips to Dorney Park, which is a huge amusement park in our coverage area. One night we picked up a male who was assaulted but refused to go with us unless his girlfriend went with him, too. We let her come because in our professional opinion she had to go. Twenty-five minutes later we were called back to the park to transport another assault victim; that was a rough day," Sarah added.

Sarah has also seen her share of vehicle accidents. There were some that were particularly tough for her to deal with. "Recently, we were called to a multi-vehicle accident where one car stopped, another hit it, and another hit that car. It was a tragic domino effect. We transported numerous patients to the hospital that day. Luckily only one person died; it could have been much worse. That still hits you hard, when anyone dies, but you learn to live with that reality, suck it up, and move on to the next call," Sarah said. But there are emotional scars that, while many may try to hide, still find their way into their psyches and can often be difficult to mitigate.

"Dealing with kids is especially scary and emotionally difficult when they are really sick or injured; it sticks with you," Sarah said. "Another call that was hard for me was when we were called to a multi-vehicle accident where one vehicle rolled over with a pregnant female, her boyfriend, and her three kids in the car. Several people were transported to the hospital, but, unfortunately, the pregnant mother perished. My heart sank, but I knew I had to keep my composure, at least until I left the scene," Sarah added.

Sarah knows first-hand that EMTs often are injured on the job, despite the perception that there is minimal risk. "People are not boxes," said Sarah, "They can be heavy and feel like dead weight so lifting them can be extremely hard on us. While it is easy to lift a one hundred-pound box with handles, bending the proper way to move a human is different. And moving them down steps is extremely dangerous. You can pull a muscle in your back, trip, and even fall on the patient," she added.

Sarah mentioned that one of her coworkers tripped on a piece of ice while jumping off of the back of an ambulance and tore his Achilles tendon. "It is just part of the job, and while we know the risks when we get into the medical field, it still is difficult when one of our own is injured, not to mention the patients we try so desperately to save," said Sarah.

An example of one call that had the potential for injuries to the EMTs was the time Sarah went on a call to lift-assist an 845-pound woman from her bedroom. The firefighters, out of necessity, had to cut a hole out of the exterior wall to allow them to get her safely out of the home. "The woman refused to get off her bed and there was nothing we could do to convince her. I suspect it was because she had a wound on her bottom," said Sarah. "They ended up hiring a flatbed truck, tied themselves with fire equipment for climbing and managed to get her bed onto the flatbed; it was quite an experience. Our ambulance was right there to assist and make sure she was medically stable before she arrived at the hospital. We had three fire companies and two ambulance companies all trying to make sure she was safe, secured, and in minimal distress," she added. "But I knew that with such a large woman, it could spell real danger for us if she fell on us or if we strained our backs trying to lift her. It is what we are trained for and hopefully we do it well—but it was still a physically exhausting day."

Then there are the psychiatric calls where EMTs are never quite sure what they will encounter or what precipitated the aberrant behavior. For example, a patient can be in a manic state from taking too many drugs, have low glucose levels, or an underlying mental health condition that would explain the behavior.

Sarah has had her share of mental health emergencies as well, and they are always among the hardest to deal with for EMTs.

"I was hit by a patient twice," Sarah said. "One was a dementia patient who had no clue where she was. I was trying to move her on the stretcher, and she swung at me and scratched my lip. While we do receive training, we are not trained enough to deal with every mental health condition, such as an agitated person coming out of a seizure or someone with a developmental delay or mood disorder. Our training cannot prepare us for every case scenario. They do not always understand that you are trying to help them, but you do the best you can to calm them down," said Sarah.

After about three years on the job, Sarah decided she wanted additional training to become a paramedic—a job requiring more rigorous medical education. With a paramedic designation, she can administer medications, insert IVs, and provide advanced life-saving measures. In 2020, she applied for the paramedic program at the George Moerkirk Emergency Medicine Institute where she and Padraic are now halfway through their year-long training course. Managing her life was difficult as a single mom, especially with a son with autism—making it even more important that she progress in her career. Fortunately, Sarah had support from her family including daily babysitting and emotional support.

During Sarah's journey from her EMT training to becoming a paramedic, she and Padraic's relationship was stronger than ever. They became engaged and within a few weeks, moved in together. They were a team in and out of the ambulance. "Padraic and I get along so well, but we do have separate ways of coping. I tend to want to talk and get out my frustrations.

He tends not to talk, and at the end of his shift gets in the shower and washes off the stresses of the day. But we do have a great system. He lets me unload for ten minutes. Then I let him tell me what he is thinking; I guess you could say we were destined to be together," said Sarah.

Sarah recalls one of her favorite times working with Padraic. "There was this one time that Padraic and I were on a shift together. We had responded to a call to help an elderly woman who said she was in no immediate distress. The next thing I knew I noticed her hitting on Padraic. 'Oh, you are so handsome,' I heard the woman say. It was so cute that the woman had no idea that Padraic and I were a couple. I just let it go on and Padraic flirted right back; he's silly that way," Sarah added.

Sarah and Padraic know first-hand the meaning of service. They have seen the worst of human nature and the best. They do not need endless accolades or invitations to White House dinners or ticker tape parades. All they need is each other, their family and friends, and the kindness of strangers.

"One day I was checking out at a local grocery store after work and still wearing my EMT uniform. I only had about six items in my cart, and I heard the man in front of me say, 'Hey, miss, please go in front of me.' 'Are you sure?' I asked. I thanked him for his kindness. I was so surprised that not only did he give me his place in line but he paid for my stuff. I am not suggesting anyone who sees an EMT should do something like that, but a simple 'thank you' would be great," Sarah said.

Sarah said that when she returned home, she realized what she and Padraic did for a living made a difference. "That felt really good," she said.

Eight

LOVE IN AN AMBULANCE: PART TWO

Of all the gin joints in all the towns in all the world, she walks into mine.
—Humphrey Bogart, as Rick Blaine in *Casablanca*

PADRAIC AND SARAH'S RELATIONSHIP BEGAN IN A CLASSROOM, BLOSSOMED into love in an ambulance, and evolved into a marriage of equals. But despite the two lovebirds' camaraderie and mutual admiration, Padraic and Sarah are not on the same page about one highlight of their relationship—the conversation about their first date.

More about that later.

Padraic Daraghy was born on July 4, 1989, into a large extended Irish Catholic family in Red Bank, New Jersey, but his time in his birthplace was short-lived. When he was only eight weeks old, his parents moved their young family to Palmer, Pennsylvania, on September 26, 1989. His mother was a home economics teacher, and his father was in the US Coast Guard. Both parents were very loving and supportive of Padraic's passions. Padraic was an affable, energetic child, always on the go—sometimes too much, according to his mother, Maggie.

And there was one time in his young life when his indefatigable energy landed him in the hospital, which Padraic believes was the genesis of his passion for medicine and helping others.

"I was at my best friend's house building a fort like many young boys were doing at the time, and I tripped on the white sheet we were using to construct our roof," Padraic said. "Somehow, I lost my balance and I fell hard breaking my left femur, from my knee to my hip," he explained.

Padraic's mother immediately called 911; the ambulance picked him up and rushed him to the hospital. On the way there, Padraic was comforted by one of the EMTs who said something that went over his head at the time, but was oddly fascinating. He told Padraic that when he was a young boy, he had his own bout with pain. "From what I recall, the EMT was a cool dude. He told me a story that happened to him—I assume because he wanted to calm me down—that he had to cut off all the toes on his right foot as a result of a lawn mower accident. Now looking back, I would have loved to see his toeless foot," Padraic joked.

Padraic arrived in the emergency room, was evaluated by the doctor on call, and then admitted to the hospital where his medical journey began. "I was in traction for two weeks with a spike cast placed above my belly button down to the bottom of my leg. The traction was terrible, especially because not only was I so young, but the problem with traction is that you have to have your legs in the air for twenty-four hours. And the worst part is that you cannot sleep because your head is down and your feet are up; it really sucked," he said.

Padraic's family did everything they could do to help. Once Padraic was able to go home—still in a cast—his mother and uncle concocted a few homemade innovations to make his life easier. For example, his uncle, who was a US Air Force veteran, gave Padraic his flight helmet. It had the same tubing as the hospital used to deliver oxygen. "It delivered air throughout the helmet instead of using a mask that moved all over my face," Padraic said. It also kept his head from bobbing around while he slept. But no matter how much Padraic's family tried to ameliorate the situation, it did leave its mark on the young boy.

"When I was in the hospital, and for some time after, I had violent nightmares. I felt like I was falling from a high building. I also was getting terrible nose bleeds. After about ten weeks I figured out if I got up on the balls of my feet, I could hobble around the house, which made me feel a bit better," said Padraic.

The doctors warned Padraic and his mother that he needed to be careful and follow their directions to a T. "They put the fear of God in me and said if I did not do what they said that I might never walk again, walk with a limp, or even find that one leg might be shorter than the other. That really freaked me out," Padraic said.

After the ordeal was over, Padraic and his mother arrived at the doctor's office to have the cast finally removed; he was thrilled. He could see his leg again and it was all in one piece. No limp. No size difference. "I was over-joyed, and when that cast was finally gone, I could not wait to get out of the doctor's office for the last time. The only hitch was that they forgot to tell me that I needed to use a walker, but of course I did not have one. As my mother and I were heading out of the office, the doctor said: 'Your son is walking unassisted and looks great. I do not think he will need meds or even physical therapy.' I was ecstatic," said Padraic.

As Padraic and his mother left the office, Padraic would soon learn how much he appreciated the experience. He was broken, but thankfully repaired, and inspired.

From that day on, Padraic would find he was fascinated by hearing about medical emergencies and watching medical shows on television. He could not get enough of them.

It was around that time, when he was in first grade, that he and his mother realized Padraic had a learning disability. He was diagnosed with dyslexia, a term for a disorder that affects a person's ability to read and inter-pret symbols, letters, and words.

He also had another learning disability called dysgraphia, which is a neu-rological disorder that causes people to use the wrong words as well as write them incorrectly. As a result, Padraic always had problems in school. Except for wood shop. That was where he excelled. "Wood shop was the place where no one could tell me what I was doing was wrong. It was tactile and mechanical and my brain was able to figure things out and do them really well," Padraic said.

He was so talented in wood shop that his teacher would recruit him to help instruct the younger students. Once he graduated high school, Padraic tried community college for general studies and Millersville University for more technical courses. But college was not in the cards; Padraic flunked out. "My mother and I had a hard conversation about my future and what I needed to do to find a career that I liked, and where I could succeed," said Padraic. After considerable reflection, Padraic decided to pursue what he did best—a career in carpentry. He was admitted to the Triangle Tech School where he studied carpentry and construction and learned how to build homes and cabinets, and also do all the "finish work."

Padraic graduated in 2012; he was twenty-two years old. But after a few job interviews he felt he was not suitable for, Padraic decided to take a job at Home Depot. He was part of the merchandise execution team, where he would rebuild displays for the company's vendors. The vendors would pay Home Depot for that service and Padraic held the position for two years.

"I was just too young and could not work at one job that long. Plus, I was bored so easily," said Padraic. "During that time, I also attended an open house at the local fire department. They said they would sponsor me to take classes if I would volunteer for them. So, I signed up." Padraic was very motivated, took numerous classes, and finally received his certification in case he decided to become a full-time firefighter.

"While I enjoyed being a firefighter, when I got a call from a concrete company I jumped at the chance, figuring I could use my technical skills and build pre-form concrete and concrete that is used in street storm drains, for example," he said.

Padraic needed to find his passion, though at times he and his mother thought that would never happen. In a stroke of good fortune that he had no idea at the time would help him find his purpose, Padraic developed a severe allergy to the chemicals in the concrete dust he was working with every day. He developed rashes and chemical burns on his legs and arms; he was done.

"Son, what do you really want to do?" Padraic's mother asked him one day when they were having breakfast.

"I do not know, Mom; maybe I should be an EMT? I like helping people, and I can do that until I figure out what I really want to do." His mother thought that was finally a solid plan and could give her son a career that he could stick with and succeed at.

Padraic took a job as a paratransit—a wheelchair driver. After doing that for a while, he finally decided to enroll in EMT school; that is where he met Sarah.

For the first time in his life, Padraic felt a sense of belonging; a place where his learning disabilities would not be that obvious. "I felt so relieved to finally find a career—not just a job—where I think I could actually have a future," said Padraic.

Padraic's EMT class was diverse, but the students clearly had different goals. "I am in a class filled with people—who I would estimate—about half are never going to use the certification to pay their bills. They get their EMT so they can go on to be a physician's assistant or attend medical school. The idea is that they have a nice base of knowledge. But with my learning disability, I had to learn in my own time," he explained.

"When I was driving an ambulance, I found I could talk to people about anything. I would ask them about their families and those conversations helped me learn how to read people. I learned to feed off of their responses to get the answers I was looking for," Padraic added. "That skill was beneficial for my future."

Sarah did the same thing. She was a wheelchair driver too. And after a few weeks in class, Sarah and Padraic became good friends. Though Sarah was six years older than Padraic, they had a lot in common. Every Sunday they would talk about the patient of the week and found they could confide in each other about the work and their bosses as well. "We enjoyed hanging out and it was a nice relief having someone like Sarah who I could relate to and bitch about work," Padraic explained.

Padraic enjoyed Sarah's enthusiasm and humor but did have an issue with Sarah's recollection of how their romance began.

"I was going to my cousin's wedding and since we are a large Irish family, weddings can take up to three days. First, we all hang out in the hotel room, then have the rehearsal dinner, the wedding, and the next day get together for breakfast," said Padraic. "I told Sarah I was not going to class and asked her if she could let me know if I missed anything? Then I sent her a text and she said, 'Pad, have a bourbon for me,'" he recalled.

When Padraic returned to class after the wedding, Sarah told him about a disturbing incident with one of their fellow students. "Pad, this guy came by and got into my personal space," she said.

"'What did you do?' I asked. 'Well, he was texting me weird messages and harassing me. Would it be okay with you if I tell him we were dating to get him off my back?'

"I thought about it for a minute and since I am a smart ass, I said, 'No way.' 'What do you mean?' she asked me, clearly shocked by my answer. I must admit for a second I was enjoying the game, but I finally gave in and asked her if she would like to go on a date. Her answer was 'yes,'" he recalled. So, while Sarah misinterpreted what Padraic was thinking, the end result was what ultimately mattered.

When Padraic and Sarah received their EMT certifications, they both eventually ended up working for Cetronia Ambulance. The company told Padraic that there were three jobs open. "The boss told me that I can work the day shift in the platoon opposite of Sarah, the night shift with Sarah, or the overnight platoon opposite Sarah. The only catch, he told me, was that if I chose to work with her that there would be 'no hanky panky' in the back of the truck. Seriously, if you have ever been in an ambulance, it is not exactly the most pleasant location in the world for romance," said Padraic.

Sarah and Padraic were partners for ten months. But the three, twelve-hour night shifts proved to be too demanding for the couple. Padraic began working with a new partner, Kris (Amy's husband from chapter 6), and that began a lifelong friendship between the two couples and colleagues.

Kris and Padraic had many things in common—a desire to help people and a fascination with medicine and emergency medicine, not to mention a wicked temper.

"When Kris and I started working together, we got same admonition from management—to watch out for the other's temper and fuse. I have all the patience in the world for people who cannot do for themselves, but not for stupid behavior. I get very annoyed at people who I must pick up who are stupid and get drunk at a bar, for example. That is stupid. But I have all the empathy in the world for a ninety-year-old man or woman that falls out of bed, or cannot urinate," Padraic explained.

Like all EMTs and paramedics, every call is different and presents a variety of challenges. Padraic explains that he has no problem responding to a call where someone at a function drinks too much and gets sick. "I have no problem showing up and giving the patient a vomit bag and telling them to sleep it off. But when they are belligerent all bets are off. That is where occasionally my issues arise," said Padraic. "While I may be a little short with some staff, I am never that way with a patient. In fact, I love going to nursing homes, because I have seen so much that I can usually know what a patient needs—for example, an elderly woman suffering from a urinary tract infection, or a man afraid because his dementia is causing him to hallucinate. I have to care why they are complaining, how they are feeling, and how I can fix the problem."

Padraic said that his early experience in the hospital and his learning disabilities helped him learn how to anticipate what people need and elicit the answers to questions that others could not. He tells the story of a woman who he was dispatched to evaluate for suicide ideation. "We showed up and the patient and police were there, but I did not know the officers since it was out of my route. Sometimes I must get the patient away from law enforcement because they can become even more stressed. I calmly explained that she could come with me willingly or I can take her against her will and have her committed. I also explained that the moment a person is involuntarily committed it appears on their record permanently," Padraic recalled.

The strategy worked. Padraic decided to probe the patient to find out if she were truly having a psychological episode or if there was something else going on. She did not appear that distressed. "Can I ask you why people thought you were acting so strangely and why they called us?" Padraic asked.

"I am not suicidal, I'm depressed," she said.

The two talked for at least an hour and the woman revealed she had two bulging discs, was in severe pain, and that her surgeon would not provide pain management because he was afraid she would become addicted to the pain medication. "Time out," Padraic said. "Let me get this straight. You are depressed because you have pain? So, this is what I am going to do. Now I realize you are not suicidal so; I can take you to the hospital and give them the real story. How does that sound?" Padraic asked.

"I cannot thank you enough, sir. No one else would have done that for me. Thank you for listening to my problem and helping me with the real one," she said.

"I do not think most people realize the full aspect of what we do. We are mobile therapists, social workers, priests, surrogate parents, and com-forters-in-chief," said Padraic. "We are the jack of all trades in the healthcare profession."

And despite their expertise, training, and tough personas, EMTs and paramedics do get emotional despite their training to compartmentalize their feelings. "Every day we lose a tiny bit of ourselves and have to find ways to cope. You could say we are a weird bunch. But we have to separate our work and life from our home and personal life, or we will go nuts," said Padraic.

That is where his love and best friend Sarah comes in. Not to mention a six-inch green stuffed dinosaur named Ray. "Sarah and I decided to bring a stuffed dinosaur we named Ray into our truck for a variety of reasons," Padraic explains. "It sounds crazy, but when we are stressed, we will make Ray talk. Ray would yell at the radio, telling dispatchers they suck or make sarcastic comments to each other. We gave Ray his own special voice," said Padraic.

"This was a stress reliever for us. Obviously, he is inanimate, but it is amazing how this simple technique works," said Padraic. "And Ray also helps the kids we treat feel less afraid during their most vulnerable times; he even makes the traumas we see every day more palatable."

Padraic and Sarah share their devotion to their profession, the people they treat, and each other. "We never imagined that we would fall in love in an ambulance," said Padraic. "I cannot imagine any other job I would rather do. Just knowing you helped someone survive and even thrive is a rush. Every day is an exciting one and having Sarah—and Ray—by my side is what makes my world better; I finally found my purpose and my forever," Padraic said.

Nine

FROM SEA TO SERVICE

Life is what happens to you while you're busy making other plans.
—John Lennon

K RIS VIERLING WAS BORN TO SERVE. THERE WAS A TIME WHEN HE thought he might work with computers, but the Navy veteran ended up having other plans. There would be no desk jobs in Kris's future. He was drawn to and fascinated by helping people when they are at their worst. Clearing an airway. Stopping a bleed. Comforting the elderly. Kris embodies all the requisite qualities to be a truly outstanding paramedic.

"I guess you could say I have been in the medical field my whole life," said Kris. "There literally is no other job in the world I would rather do. And even at forty-seven when most of the people I know are burnt out, I am still running on all cylinders."

Kris was born in Allentown, Pennsylvania in 1974. His father worked at Bethlehem Steel Company and was a crane operator. His parents separated when he was fifteen and Kris went to live with his mother in California, only to return to Pennsylvania six months later. His mother stayed in California and tragically died of leukemia in 1991, when Kris was just seventeen years old. "It was rough. It was only two years after they divorced that my mom died, and it hit me hard," said Kris. "It was a double whammy. First my parents divorced and then my mom died. My brother Bryon, who was five years older than me, was already out of the house and in the Navy. My next eldest brother Kenny was still at home living with Pop," he added.

At the time, there was no money for Kris to attend college, though he would have loved to have had that academic experience. Still, he needed to get out of the house and find a job as a fallback. "I realized that if I were not going to go to college, I had to do something," Kris explained. "So, when I was a junior in high school, I signed up for the Navy's delayed entry program and was accepted. As soon as I graduated, I was off to boot camp in San Diego, California," Kris added.

Kris was well prepared for beginning his medical career in the US Navy. When he was a high school sophomore, he was certified in advanced first aid and had some emergency medical training as well. So, following his basic training, he took a three-month course and worked in a hospital with the goal of becoming a Navy Corpsman with combat medic training. "I loved learning as much about trauma as I could," said Kris. "Unlike civilian medicine, we were trained for treating severe trauma—things like stopping bleeding from someone who stepped on an improvised explosive device (IED), stabilizing broken bones, treating head injuries, or keeping gaping wounds from becoming infected. I was ready to go anywhere the Navy planned to send me, and I felt my training was top-notch," he added.

It was during this time that Kris, just nineteen years old, met his first wife, Tanya, also in the Navy and in the same Corpsman program. After dating for only three months, the couple was married. The only problem was that Tanya was sent to the Sandpoint Navy Shipyard in Washington State—three states away from her new husband. Kris applied for spousal co-location orders and soon was able to pack up his belongings and join Tanya to begin their new life together.

"I got a job at the Bremerton Naval Hospital and was essentially doing the same work as the nurses," said Kris. "But since I was enlisted and was not an officer, the nurses had to make sure I did not make mistakes," Kris explained. "But my training was so good that I think everyone trusted me and it was a very enjoyable experience."

From there, Kris spent one year in a medical clinic at the Bremerton Naval Shipyard where he treated retired and active-duty military members and civilians. "Shipyard clinics may not seem like places where there are many injuries, but that could not be further from the truth," Kris said. "The ship workers mainly worked on decommissioned submarines, and they had many injuries due to gashes from cutting through steel, stepping on sharp objects, and receiving severe burns. After about three years in the Navy, I made the decision to leave the military with the goal of working full-time in a hospital," Kris added.

Kris was honorably discharged in 1996 and Tanya in 1997. By this time, they had a one-year-old child, Kile, while they were living in Evert, Washington.

The young family drove across the country—from Washington State to Emmaus, Pennsylvania where Kris got a job at Lehigh Valley Hospital, where he worked from 1997 to 2003 in a variety of positions. During their time in Pennsylvania, Kris and Tanya had two other children—Del and Angelique.

But despite Kris doing well at the hospital, he became restless. Something was missing. He realized that his combat and trauma training were not being utilized as much as he'd hoped, so Kris decided it was time to make another change. However, since Kris's EMT certification had expired, he was required to take the class again while still working at the hospital and volunteering for the local ambulance company. Kris thought he could bide his time until a full-time job opened up.

Kris was also motivated to make the career change so he could save enough money to support his young family. Fortunately, it was not that long before he received a job offer from a local ambulance company, and he jumped at the chance to work for them.

"I was thrilled that the Emmaus Ambulance Corps hired me, and I worked for them from 2003 to 2009. They were a great organization and they even let me take my paramedic training classes while I was working as an EMT; three years later I became an official paramedic," said Kris.

After six years and a vast amount of EMS experience, Kris decided to approach Cetronia Ambulance for a potential paramedic position. Cetronia had a great reputation, and now that Kris was a paramedic, he believed that would help him advance his career and give him additional EMS experience.

Kris was assigned to the ALS (Advanced Life Support) ambulance, and also the company's mobile stroke unit. (This unit has a portable CT scanner on board that enables the crew to detect strokes early.) This was right up Kris's alley. In addition, since Cetronia is the largest ambulance company in the region, they have contracts with many organizations.

* * *

Continuing his passion for diverse service, Kris joined the Pennsylvania EMS Strike Team in 2010. This is the group that gets deployed all across the country for natural or man-made disasters. In 2012, Super Storm Sandy ravaged the East Coast; it was among the most deadly and destructive storms during that hurricane season. The storm surge and wall of water that breached the shoreline caused forty-nine deaths in New York and ten in New Jersey, destroyed hundreds of homes, and made it the deadliest storm in the region since 1972. Kris traveled to New Jersey for nine days to help rescue victims and assist in all aspects of the rescue and recovery.

"We ran emergency calls twenty-four hours a day to help residents who were trapped in their homes or were in imminent danger. We also took care of elderly persons that were taken to the middle school for safety reasons," Kris explained.

First responders such as Kris are, at their core, humanitarians who just happen to know a great deal about healthcare.

"As an EMT, I always loved prehospital care. I got to see people at their worst, and I knew I could help them despite their injuries. I found it more interesting going into their homes than just working in a hospital setting. I especially enjoyed treating the elderly. They are normally so grateful we are there," said Kris.

Even though Kris had military combat training, he realized over time that he was not a "trauma junkie."

"I did not need to see blood and guts. For me, helping people, no matter what their injury, was the most rewarding part of the job."

Over time, and with some excellent partners, Kris became a seasoned provider and someone confident in his abilities and judgements. He always wanted to know more and found he could assess a situation and make an informed judgment quickly. "People sometimes think that all symptoms are the same," said Kris, "but that is furthest from the truth. Every chest pain, every breathing difficulty, or high or low blood pressure is different. I must assess the level of pain and distress and make a split decision as to what I need to treat first. For example, I had a patient who told me his pain level was a 'ten' but then he proceeded to tell me a dirty joke. Another patient said their pain level was a 'three' but they were crying hysterically; I had to learn how to read my patients better and watch for the subtle clues and symptoms," Kris explained.

Kris said it is important as a paramedic to triage the injury and treat the most critical one first. "If someone has a fractured neck and moves the wrong way, that could be serious. I have to stabilize the patient's neck first, but if he also has broken ankle that can wait. The ankles heal. I can get to them next. You have to treat a life-threatening condition right away. Nothing else matters if they cannot breathe, or if you cannot stop their bleeding. That is where our training comes in to make a quick assessment, treat the life-threatening issues first, then tackle the small stuff," Kris added.

Kris said that people often ask him, "'How do you care for a patient in a moving ambulance?' That is certainly challenging and dangerous on its own. We do have seat belts but sometimes we must remove them—only when it is absolutely necessary," Kris explained. "We reach for equipment, stick IVs in patients, and even perform CPR all while moving fast and maneuvering around turns. It is extremely hard at times and as the saying goes, we have to develop 'legs.' You could say we ride the waves and potholes of the road," Kris said.

Patients who are taken by ambulance to the hospital are grateful. But not the "entitled" ones, Kris explained. "I can honestly say that I love my patients. Most are so thankful we are there for them, and it is those folks that make me happy and want to do this job forever," said Kris. "But it is the people who feel entitled—who honestly believe that life owes them—that make me crazy. Unbelievably, there have been patients that were so obnoxious that they would say things such as, 'Why did you take so long to get to me?' 'Where is my blanket?' or 'Why is there no pillow on my stretcher?' I learned over the years to keep my cool, stay friendly, and always be as nice as I can despite my personal feelings."

And then there are the "frequent flyers." Kris explained that there are people who call 911 every week, sometimes every day. They like to be seen at the hospital, and Kris believes they are lonely, troubled, or need attention. "We are not allowed to refuse a 911 call," said Kris. "In Pennsylvania, we have to respond to these folks no matter how many times we have to pick them up. I just smile, work hard to hide my feelings, and treat them with dignity and respect. Then I'll complain to my partner after the call is over," Kris said.

"It amazes me that these entitled patients think we always have to do what they say. They are in control, not us. They think it is our fault that they have the problems they have," Kris said. "There was once a call we responded to from a five-hundred-pound man who was indignant when we said we needed to call a lift assist to get him to the hospital. He was yelling and screaming at us and had no concern for our well-being or safety. If we were to lift him by ourselves, we could have really hurt backs or even been crushed by the man if he fell on us while we were lifting him," Kris recalled.

* * *

Kris said he's also had guns pointed at him and his partner at least three or four times in his career. "This usually happens when a family member calls for an ambulance but does not tell the dispatcher that it is a psych patient needing help. My military training helps in these situations. I try to talk them down the best I can. And if I do need law enforcement, I call them on our radios, though the emergency buttons do not always work, especially inside an apartment building. I always tell people, this is not a job for the faint of heart," said Kris.

Most people do not realize that EMTs and paramedics have a high injury and suicide rate. "Injury-wise we are always climbing in and out of cars, carrying heavy individuals during many difficult rescue situations, and slipping on wet and icy roads, as just a few examples," Kris explained. "I have known a colleague who was traumatized when he saw a young girl hanging from a window blind cord in her bedroom; he quit on the spot. Child abuse cases, bad traumas from gang violence can also break people. While there is professional help available to us, some guys just will not admit they have a problem. I believe toxic masculinity is one of the reasons," he added.

Fortunately, for Kris, there were only a couple of times that affected him emotionally. "I went on a call where a tractor trailer hit a vehicle with three people in the car. The two people in the front seat were young and did not sustain any serious injuries, but when we pulled out the person in the back of the car, it was an older lady who was crushed and deceased. I kept seeing her lifeless body every night before I went to sleep. I had insomnia for a week straight and had to call the CISM team—Critical Incident Stress Management—and that helped," Kris said.

* * *

For all of the stress and trauma EMTs and paramedics experience every day, there are many moments of joy. "There was one time I saved a man with cardiac arrest during Thanksgiving. The next thing I knew, his family brought me a giant basket of fruit," said Kris. "Other than the goodies and kind letters sent to our management, my favorite acts of gratitude are when

Grandpa falls in his home, and after we get there and help him up, Grandma gives us a big kiss. It is just human nature that if patients are friendly, we are nicer to them as well. Sure, we always will give them that extra pillow or a warm blanket. But when they are mean or are drunk or on drugs, we bite our tongues. Nevertheless, we will always do our best to save their lives and treat them professionally. But we do love our grandmas!" Kris explained.

And then there are the life experiences that Kris believes were exhilarating. "For a couple of years, I was assigned to the squad that provided emergency medical services to Pocono Raceway," Kris said. The superspeedway is located in the Pocono Mountains in Pennsylvania and hosts two annual NASCAR Cup races and other racing events as well.

"We are contracted to provide ambulance coverage for Pocono Raceway," Kris said. "NASCAR requires us to have extra training to work on the racetrack. And there are two positions for EMS crews there—infield and track. I only worked on the track. It is a lot more fun to be able to see the race from that perspective and help people in case of accidents or sudden illness," Kris added.

"When you are working a major race as a paramedic, you can be assigned to three basic areas of the venue—the pit, the track, and the stands. We are trained for all emergencies that could occur, and we need to know a good deal about the cars as well. I have had to provide medical aid to a number of fans, some of the pit crew members, and thankfully rarely, a couple of the drivers. But it never fails. When you are at Pocono it is beyond exciting watching these powerful vehicles driving the course at speeds in excess of 150 miles per hour. I guess you could say that it is one of the few perks of the job as far as excitement goes," Kris explained.

And then there are the disasters. Kris volunteered to be part of Cetronia's disaster team, which is akin to being in the reserves in the military. When there are major disasters in the United States, ambulance companies such as Kris's are contracted by the government to be dispatched to the scene. Employees are not obligated to participate in the disaster team, but for Kris it was a "no brainer."

"I was one of the first to sign up," Kris said, "and it just felt like the right thing to do."

Among the most memorable, yet tragic, for Kris was when he was dispatched to help rescue people trapped in their homes during Hurricane Katrina in August 2005. This Category 5 Atlantic Hurricane hit New Orleans hard and caused more than 1,800 deaths due to high winds reaching

175 miles per hour and extreme flooding. "When we first arrived in New Orleans, it felt like a gut punch. We had to move quickly to rescue people from their flooded homes and streets," Kris said.

Yet, after a fulfilling career as an EMT and paramedic, Kris's personal life was not proceeding as planned. After twenty-seven years of marriage, Kris and Tanya were divorced—though they remained good friends. "Tanya is a great person, but we are not great together," Kris said.

After the divorce, Kris decided to go on the Facebook dating site, and there he met the love of his life, Amy. The next morning, he left a message for Amy and the two planned a date at a local pizza restaurant. That was one year ago and since that time they were inseparable; they were married in June 2021.

"Amy and I have so much in common. She was also an EMT, so she knows what I am going through and understands me completely. Amy is actually interested in what I do each day and is my best friend," said Kris.

* * *

Now that Kris has found the love of his life, and a career he relishes, he has no plans of retiring anytime soon. He plans to defy the odds and continue to be a paramedic well into his fifties. "I figure I have ten more years as a paramedic, and why should I retire if I am healthy and still love my job?" he asked. "I may not have enough money saved to be able to go to Europe or buy that Mercedes, but I am content with my life; I do not need a lot of money to be happy," he said.

Kris always encourages young people to consider a career as an EMT or paramedic. "People always need help," Kris explained. "This is a great field. Once I take young people on ride-alongs, they can see firsthand how fulfilling and rewarding the job is. Plus, we are all getting older and I am hoping that these kids will at some point be able to take care of me and all of us who are aging," said Kris.

"Life has a way of making other plans for you, but I am a better man for the choices I made. I can sleep at night knowing that I have helped others during the most trying times of their lives; that is all the reward I need," Kris said.

Ten

MAN ON A MISSION

Life's most persistent and urgent question is: What are you doing for others?
—Martin Luther King Jr.

D AVID SHEATS HAS A PASSION FOR SERVICE. HE NEVER WANTED TO SIT behind a desk, trade securities, own a grocery store, or manage an automobile agency. Instead, his career led him in a multitude of directions—all involving saving lives and keeping his community safe.

One of the first experiences that David realized motivated him to become a first responder was when he was a teenager living in Howard, Pennsylvania, a rural county with the closest city, Lock Haven, about twenty miles away. They lived in a small mobile home with few amenities other than an addition that his father built to accommodate the young family including his sister, his mother, and father. "My dad was rather strict. My sister and I had to do our share of chores, but otherwise it was a wonderful place to grow up," David said. "I played baseball for most of my childhood and adolescence, and when I got older rode my motorcycle; I actually believed that most people lived just the way we did."

When David was fifteen years old, his idyllic view of the world was shattered.

For most of his career, David's father worked for the Hammermill Paper Company in Lock Haven, Pennsylvania. One day while he was at work, David and his family were all sleeping when they smelled smoke coming from the fireplace chimney. The fire was billowing through the walls.

"We called 911, and my mother started hollering at the dispatcher to get the fire department here right away," David said.

"When the firefighters showed up with all of their gear, they quickly pulled out the fire hose and started breaking in through the walls with axes," David recalled. "While I was a wreck and realized we could have all been killed had the fire spread to our mobile home, I was also fascinated. So much so, that a few days after the fire, I told my dad I wanted to join the firehouse."

That fire was the springboard for the rest of David's emerging life of service.

So, at sixteen, David became a junior firefighter. He soon discovered that the firefighters he met there were akin to a brotherhood, and found his core group who offered their wisdom, advice, and training. "When you are a junior firefighter, all you can do is learn about the profession and not actually go out on calls," said David. "You basically learn everything that is literally on the firetruck. The hoses, ladders, and all the gauges. I was a quick study, and it was not long before the other firefighters recognized I knew what I was doing. But I was still in high school at that point and thinking that all I wanted to be [was] a firefighter."

"In my senior year—and just in case it did not work out as a firefighter—I was in the process of taking graphic arts and photography courses while still volunteering at the fire station. One of the firefighters mentioned to me that they were offering free EMT classes, so I decided to take them up on the offer," David recalled.

Now just seventeen years old, David passed the EMT course, and by chance had a career course correction—one that would give him a new challenge and the ability to help others. "A buddy of mine moved to Lehigh Valley, Pennsylvania and was working for an ambulance company there. I was surprised that he offered me a job with his company. But I was always up for a challenge and so I accepted his offer right away," David said.

David met his friend for the weekend in Easton, Pennsylvania—that was where the ambulance company was headquartered—and the two discussed the details of the job. David signed up on the spot.

But his father was not thrilled. Coming from such a small town, with little of the benefits of city life, he had no trouble voicing his disapproval. "David, you have to do what is best for you but you will not last three months in the city, I guarantee you," said his father. David realized that his father was concerned that, as country kid who only knew baseball all of his life, he would have trouble adjusting. That could not have been further from the truth.

Suburban Emergency Medical Services was David's first paid job. He was just eighteen years old. "I was called to help people who were in auto accidents at the time—many of whom were trapped in their vehicles. When I look back, I realize how that experience helped me to grow up quickly, but I also learned one important lesson. That everything was not always about me," David said. "Some people wearing a uniform do their jobs for selfish reasons and are impressed with all of the patches up and down their sleeves. I am my most satisfied when I know I am helping someone—period!" he added.

As most EMTs will attest, they see the worst of human nature, yet have the rare opportunity to turn a tragedy into a triumph—or at least mitigate a life-threatening situation. As a young EMT, David worked literally thousands of night shifts, where there would be recurring severe auto accidents and other unexpected emergencies. "I was working in Palmer Township and in the Wilson Borough where we had a section of the Glendon Bridge, which had four-lanes that on one side appeared that there was a river below. But in fact, it was an eighty-foot drop on pure concrete. We would frequently get calls to rescue people jumping off the bridge who thought they would be falling into a body of water," said David.

David said that working on an ambulance with a good partner is an important lifeline for dealing with stress and the traumatic nature of the job. "No matter the call, you have to answer it and it can be especially hard when you have to help a child that was hit by a car. Having a partner that I trust completely is critical in our jobs as EMTs. As a team we are given a responsibility to help everyone and when they are hurting, we always let them know we are doing everything to save their lives. Calls like that can take a toll on you. They can be exceedingly difficult to emotionally overcome," David added.

David, and most of his colleagues, usually know right away if a young EMT will make it or not in the field. It is not a job for the faint of heart. "You not only have to deal with lots of actual blood and gruesome scenes, but sometimes it is multiple times a day," David explained. "There was one time that a new EMT was with me on a call for a victim who was shot numerous times. When we arrived on the scene he threw up and ran outside of the truck, yelling, 'I cannot do this!' 'Why do you think you cannot do it?' I asked." The young man never answered David. He got in his car, drove away, and was never heard from again.

After twelve years on the job and treating thousands of people—from children and their parents to the elderly and young men and women—David has seen it all. Broken bones, broken hearts, drug overdoses, heart attacks, gunshot wounds, falls, or someone just needing a helping hand to get up. Nevertheless, being a firefighter and then an EMT was David's dream job and life's calling.

But there was still much more he wanted to do.

By this time, David was married and had two boys—Michael and Joseph. He loved being a father, but soon realized that money was becoming an issue. So, when he was offered a job working in the City of Bethlehem's 911 Call Center, he jumped at the opportunity to supplement his income. (In 2001, EMTs were earning $13 per hour. Paramedics were making a bit more.)

While not being in the field took some adjustment for David, he soon realized his EMT training was a plus. He could help a caller in an emergency—not only to calm down but also he could give them the kind of instructions he knew would work in the real world. This is called the Emergency Medical Dispatch (EMD) training course that is required for all dispatchers. And with seventy thousand residents in David's service area, and because of his vast experience and expertise, he lasted in that job for seventeen years. "It was easier for me understand without being there. For example, if someone were having trouble breathing, I knew what questions to ask and used my field experience," he explained. "I would tell the caller to lean forward. It would take the pressure off the victim's diaphragm so they would not have to excessively breathe. And I would be giving them instructions as long as it took until the prehospital personnel arrived."

"I thought being a dispatcher would remove the emotional element of the job but that never happened. There was one time I had a call about a young man lying in the backyard of his house and not breathing. That hit me hard because at the time my son was the same age," David said. "It also bothered me because his dad was hysterical and not listening to me. I knew what to do, but I could not relay that to the dad. I told him, 'Please, you have to let me help you to open his airway, so he will not choke.' He was not listening to what I was telling him one bit. 'Sir, you have to listen to me,' I kept telling him over and over. He was hysterical. All he could say was, 'Come on, buddy, wake up, wake up buddy,'" David lamented.

"Paramedics arrived on the scene, and I asked someone to please take my radio. *I could have done something to help that young man. Why did his father not listen to me?* I thought. I was crushed."

"The next thing I knew, my captain called me over and said, 'You are done for the day.' That is when I talked to our critical response team and that helped. Weeks later the boy's father showed up at our office and wanted to meet me. He thanked me for trying to save his son's life and told me he died of a congenital heart disease that no one in his family knew he had. I was touched that he reached out but saddened at the same time," said David.

When David would walk into a home as an EMT he would see people at their lowest points. He knew what to do. On the phone, his primary goal was to be compassionate and patient, knowing the person making that 911 call was not. "When someone calls us, they are generally yelling and screaming, and we have to know where they are to send help. I would say, 'Ma'am, stop, I need to know where you are. If we cannot find you, we cannot help you.' Back then there was no enhanced 911 as there is today," David explained.

As a 911 dispatcher, David might receive forty to fifty calls a night. Not all of them were emergency calls, as one might imagine. "I have had calls saying that a pregnant woman's water has broken, their electricity was not working, or their mailbox was vandalized," David recalled. "This one guy called in while sitting at an ice cream shop across from the local high school. He stated he saw three hooded males with guns run into the high school. It was believed to be an active shooter situation, so they had to lock down the school for the rest of the day. Then, they set up a perimeter command post for safety. Finally, the police tracked down the caller by tracing the call back to a prepaid cell that was purchased at the local Walmart. The informant used a credit card to pay for it. Bad choice on his part. He was arrested and was taken to jail," David said.

Despite the challenging calls, and years of dealing with the stress of the job, this never deterred David from his love of helping others. "People rely on me and even if I am tired from the day before, I go on to the next call. No one enters this field without that sense of purpose. We all ascribe to a higher standard; that is who I am as well," said David.

During his tenure as a 911 dispatcher, he met another EMT from New York City who was one of the first responders on the scene after the terrorist attacks on 9/11. He noticed David's height—he was six foot one with a large, imposing figure, and said: "You are a big guy, have you ever considered being a bounty hunter or bail bondsman?" David was intrigued. He did some research, decided that was a good idea, and enrolled in the National Institute of Bail Enforcing, which David thought would provide excellent training. However, during this process he changed his mind and decided becoming a constable was more appealing regardless of the fact he would need additional training.

What is a constable anyway? Most people confuse the role of a constable with a police officer—but there is a significant difference. Constables have their roots in the Roman Empire where they were responsible for keeping horses for the monarchs. Today, most constables are law enforcement officers, but can have different duties depending on the jurisdictions where they operate. In the United States, they are elected or appointed and are considered "peace officers," executing bench warrants and arresting violators, but not able to respond to crimes in progress, conduct traffic stops, or arrest suspects.

"It took me six months of additional training to become a constable. I would attend classes on Friday, Saturday, and Sunday," David said. "I loved learning about this aspect of law enforcement and using my skills as an EMT and 911dispatcher to my advantage."

Dealing with people at their worst became David's specialty. He knew how to handle every aspect of a person's distress and was not afraid to confront even the scariest of individuals in his new role as constable. He dealt with everything from warrants for unpaid parking tickets to homicides. He also worked with smaller police departments and five different magistrates, which made David's job much easier.

"It is funny, even to me, that even now I am still nervous when I go on a call," David said. "But my training kicks in, and I treat every warrant as an EMS call which gives me confidence. When I walk up to your house in full uniform and the star badge on my chest, you will know why I am there and generally I have the control."

David believes that no matter the multitude of issues with the offender, he should treat them equally and with respect. Over time, he has built a rapport with repeat offenders. He even has served warrants on the children of those offenders. "You could say in my line of work that it can be a sorry family affair. They know that when I have to cuff them, they are going with me one way or another, and that makes my job a lot easier," David said.

One of David's tricks of the trade is to unleash his kindness gene. "When I am serving a warrant, I try to put as much honey before the rock salt. I am not there to judge, and I do not take things personally. It is a separation of church and state for me. And like I did as an EMT, I protect my defendant just as I did my partner," he explained.

David knows that once he gets the offender in his car, he explains that he is there to serve a warrant and not listen to the details of their case. It is his way of not making any judgments and keeping the person as comfortable as they can be given where they are headed.

"People I pick up multiple times tend to remember who I am by how I treated them. That makes me feel good. They allowed me to earn their respect, not demand it. And it works for me because fundamentally all people deserve a second chance," David explained.

Then there was the time that David and the barrel of a gun became too close for comfort. And it would not be the only time he would face this danger in his career as a constable.

"The first time I noticed someone with a gun on them was shocking. It was in Allentown, and I was driving up Sixth Street looking for the guy I was going to serve, and he took off running. I ran after him and when I caught up to him, he turned around and went to grab the gun in his pants. I used all of my training to calmly tell him, 'Hey, man, don't do it.' When someone points a gun at you, you do not know if it is a nerf toy or a real gun. You just see a barrel that looks like a tunnel staring at you," David explained. David admonished the man again to drop his gun and put his hands behind his back. Luckily, he did. He was cuffed and taken to jail.

But that first experience took its toll. David could not sleep for days. "In my mind I thought, *this cannot really be happening, what if he pulled the gun out?!*"

David added that most of his warrants go smoothly and without incident. "We had a young man we were picking up for a criminal mischief warrant. We had a picture of him and went to his house to serve the warrant. Of course, I knew what he looked like but when I asked him if he was Christopher, he denied it was him. I said, 'Yea you are.' He turned around and tried to get away. He was a skinny, wiry guy and here I am big guy trying to get him into custody. But when he reached for my partner's gun, we had to Taser him in his leg. He was, unfortunately, wearing nylon shorts, and the Taser was clicking meaning it was not connecting. Suddenly some of the probes stuck on his leg; I was done," David said.

The first thing David did was get him in the car, grab his med kit, and pull the darts out of his leg and apply disinfectant to the wounds. "Are you okay?" David asked the man.

He was clearly shocked. "You are kidding me, right? You mean you care that I do not get infected?" he asked.

"That is my job, son. I need to make sure you are okay," David replied.

Helping people stay alive and thrive is more than just a job for this career EMT, firefighter, 911 dispatcher, and constable. It is more than just a calling. It is an existential part of David's world view. "I look at my work as saving generations. If you cannot save a limb of a tree the forest will fall," David explains. "When I help save a house, a life, or a person from being a lifelong criminal, and they go on to becoming a productive member of society, that makes me feel the best. Their lives, for that moment in time, are partially in my hands. It is never about me but about the future. We sometimes forget that being a good human being is not a right but a responsibility. And it is one I gladly take," David said.

David is passing along his passion for service to Michael and Joseph, both of whom are junior firefighters and share their father's dedication to making the world a healthier and safer place. "I was an open book at our house. I educated my kids on the realities of life and its potential terrible consequences. My job as a dad and law enforcement officer is to show them that the world can be quite different than what they think it is," David explained. "My boys are my world and I want to teach them to be good men. That is the best thing any parent can do."

PART THREE

AMERICA'S FIREFIGHTERS

Eleven

CAPTAIN ELVIS

It's not how much you have that makes people look up to you. It's who you are.
—Elvis Presley

THERE ARE HUNDREDS OF THOUSANDS OF ELVIS PRESLEY IMPERSON-
ators around the world. Those who are recognized as Elvis Tribute
artists, as well as Elvis hopefuls that appear at festivals, wedding
chapels, cruise ships, hotels, and many other venues. They even have
their own convention comprised of other Elvis impersonators. But there
is only one Elvis impersonator that entertains wounded warriors every
Christmas at Walter Reed National Military Medical Center in Bethesda,
Maryland, and is a retired North Carolina firefighter. Meet Captain John
(Woody) Woodall—a man on a mission. A man of deep faith who has
dedicated his life to helping wounded warriors and veterans get back on
their feet. A man who after 9/11 brought his men and women to Ground
Zero to assist in recovering the remains of his fellow firefighters and
raised $7 million, along with all North Carolina firefighters, to help the
families of the fallen. He is an artist, entertainer, and philanthropist. A
firefighter who never stopped caring and dedicating his life to the service
of others.

People have often asked Woody what motivated him to put on his rhinestone bell bottoms, black wig, and lamb chop sideburns, and sing his heart
out for a group of severely injured military members and their families at
Walter Reed.

"There was a time in my life when I was in a real dark place and something came along at just the right time to give me the boost I needed," said Woody. "I always had a good voice and enjoyed singing, but I have never been asked to sing in public until my grandmother gave me an offer on the telephone I could not refuse," he added.

At the same time, Woody's friends, who were members of a four-part harmony group, came to visit him at his home in Raleigh, North Carolina. "They asked me if I wanted all of their extra amplifiers, microphones, and other equipment they used for their performances. I asked one of the guys, 'Why do you want to give me all of your equipment? Are you sure?' All he said was, 'Woody, we want you to have everything. We really do.' I was on cloud nine," Woody recalled.

Three days later, Woody went to visit his grandmother at her rest home, and she filled him in on the details of her plan. "Son, we are going to have a party on Elvis's birthday. We want you to dress like Elvis and sing a few songs," she said. Woody's facial expression gave away his hesitation and disbelief. "Look, Woody, I am your grandma, so will you do that for me?" How could he refuse?

"Okay, Grandma, I will do it, but I have no idea how the show will turn out. But I will do my best," Woody said.

At the time, Woody was twenty-nine and just beginning his career as a firefighter. Since finances were an issue, he decided to visit the local costume shop and see if he could barter with the owner for an affordable Elvis costume. He saw one that would fit the bill. It came complete with the dark wig, white rhinestone shirt with fringe, and matching tight pants. Woody thought that would be perfect for his first performance ever as an Elvis impersonator. And since he only had two months before the show at the rest home, he had to decide on his costume that day.

"How much would it cost to rent the Elvis costume?" Woody asked the store owner.

"It will be seventy-five bucks sir," the man told Woody.

"Look, I am just a firefighter, and I am volunteering at a rest home so can you give me a break?" he asked, not having a clue if he would help him out.

"I will tell you what," he told Woody, "I will sell you the entire costume for 150 bucks. How does that sound?" Woody shook the man's hand; they had a deal. Woody left the store with his glitzy costume and black wig; Elvis had arrived!

What Woody's grandmother failed to mention at the time was that the show at the rest home on Elvis' birthday was slated for one hour, not the twenty minutes that Woody assumed. He was consumed with fear—after all, he only knew about three Elvis songs by heart, and he had little time to prepare. "I really had to step up my game, but I was ready. I had to do it for Grandma," Woody recalled. "Luckily, I appreciated Elvis's gospel and sweetheart music, so I memorized the songs I liked the most and timed my performance to meet my grandma's one hour show request," he added.

It was show time! Woody arrived at the rest home with his equipment and music box in tow. The box played the songs that Woody chose for the show without any lyrics. The rest was up to him. "I was all dressed up but feeling weird and more like a clown than an Elvis impersonator. But I was giving it all I got," said Woody.

As Woody, replete in his rhinestone costume, black wig, and homegrown lamb chop sideburns, walked out to the makeshift stage, he was floored. His grandmother, it turned out, was also a persuasive promoter and unbeknownst to him, she contacted every television and radio station as well as all the local newspapers in the county. Since it was Elvis's birthday, they all showed up. "No pressure," Woody said. "All of a sudden, I am singing my heart out, and I must say, I did surprisingly well. Grandma was happy and that was my goal," he added.

Elvis was in the house! The next thing Woody knew, he was asked to perform everywhere. In fact, he was paid $1,500 for his first "professional" gig. "I bought a new costume and decided to do it right. And the more shows I performed, the better I got. If you would have asked me years ago if I would be wearing a rhinestone jumpsuit, I would say you were nuts!" said Woody.

In addition to performing in the Raleigh area, and later in his career in New York City and Washington, DC, among other cities, Woody had a novel idea. He decided to use some of the most popular Elvis songs such as "Heartbreak Hotel," "Don't be Cruel," and "Jailhouse Rock" and replace the lyrics with messages for teaching kids about fire safety. Lyrics such as, "If your clothes catch on fire, just so you know, you get on the on the floor and you roll baby roll," for example. Jim Long, the North Carolina fire commissioner—who is also the state insurance commissioner—supported Woody's idea and this became a much-anticipated program every year during Fire Prevention Week.

What motivated this twenty-nine-year-old firefighter to get into the profession in the first place and care so much about the people in his community and beyond? He credits his father, a Baptist minister, for showing him the importance of serving others, not just in word but deed. "I grew up in Garner, North Carolina, just outside of Raleigh. My dad, Emerson Woodall, was a huge influence in my life and showed me the power of faith and why it is so important to help your neighbor," Woody recalled. "I remember as a kid the lure of wanting to be a firefighter when a little girl on my block set her grass on fire. I knew how to call the fire department, so I did. Since I could not describe the exact location of the fire, I asked them to meet me at the local gas station. When they arrived, they told me to hop on the fire truck and together we drove to the fire; I was hooked," said Woody.

Woody's dream of becoming a firefighter never abated. After graduating from Wake Community College in 1975, Woody took a high-paying job working at a sprinkler company as a steam pipe welder and then became the shop foreman. By then he was married with two children and was building his dream house in Raleigh. "One day I met a Raleigh firefighter and told him of my interest in becoming a firefighter, and he convinced me to join. I knew it would be a tough process since they would only hire thirty-five firefighters out of three thousand applications. My chances were slim to none," Woody said. But Woody was in excellent shape and it turns out his father and the fire commissioner at the time were deacons together at the same church. So, Woody applied and was one of the thirty-five people who were hired.

In May 1980, Woody began the rigorous training to become a professional firefighter. Not only did he have to learn all the firefighting techniques at the state academy but he had to pass the EMT test as well. Since a firefighter's role may overlap with other first responders such as police and emergency medical professionals, the knowledge base is important. "I learned everything I could about the job as well as being an EMT. In fact, anyone who failed the EMT course was sent home. I was not about to be one of those people," Woody said.

Woody's first assignment was Station Four in Raleigh. "I was so fortunate," Woody said. "My first captain was the finest Christian I have ever met in my life. His name was Captain Ben Dickson and every day he would do something for someone in need. He used to keep five gasoline cans at all times in the trunk of his car because he said, 'You never know who needs help.'"

Woody recalls an instance when Ben helped a young man from New Hampshire who told him his mother had died and he ran out of money to get to the funeral home in Charlotte in time for the service. Ben called the cab company, paid for the fare, and then had the cab take him to the bus terminal where he paid for the ticket to take him to Charlotte. There were no paybacks ever mentioned.

There was another time when a tall redheaded kid with freckles came into the station picking his teeth with a single edge razor. "Sir, I am hungry and have not eaten in two weeks," he told Ben. That was all Ben needed to hear. "At the time, we were about to serve dinner. I will never forget that meal. We had baby beef liver, onions and gravy, peas, and fresh-baked bread," Woody said. "Ben put on his apron and served him like he was a customer in a restaurant. The young man gobbled up all the food and even ate half of the loaf of bread. The next thing we knew Ben called the Raleigh rescue mission and asked them if they had an extra bed so the young man could get a good night's sleep," said Woody.

Ben never heard from the young man again. But watching Ben for most of his career, Woody learned the meaning of charity and credits him for making him the firefighter he would eventually become. "Man, I learned so much from him. It was amazing to me that when Ben retired, no one else ever came by the station again. He made such a difference in how I treated other people. He was an angel on this earth," Woody explained.

Woody would emulate Ben throughout his storied career. During Woody's first time on a fire call, he found a man lying in the yard after mowing his grass. He was not breathing and had no pulse. After the EMTs and paramedics arrived on the scene and worked on him, Woody rode with the victim to the hospital where, thankfully, he survived. "I was so thrilled that the man and his wife came by the station three weeks later and thanked us. I thought about Ben and realized that being a firefighter is the coolest job ever, and what I learned from Ben about compassion made all the difference," Woody explained.

Woody said that if his first experience were not a positive one, he would have had a tougher time with the losses. And there were losses. "You learn to lean on the victories to help you get through the losses," said Woody. In 1982, Woody and his team arrived at a fire in Raleigh where dense smoke was billowing out of every orifice. Woody could not find the fire and the smoke was puffing and puffing. They cleared the house and found no fire. "My chief set the ladder up and I climbed up the twenty-four-foot extension. I took my axe before hooking my legs in the ladder. I was getting ready to enter the building, but the smoke was sucking back. I knew through my training about how back draft explosions happen. The next thing I knew the explosion blew me over a chain-link fence and into a neighbor's yard. I was lucky my legs were not locked into the ladder. As I lay on the ground, I knew I should not move from my EMT training, and that moving could make any injury sustained much more severe. I went to the hospital and was okay. It could have been much worse," Woody admitted. Later that night Woody was back at the station, cooking supper for his fellow firefighters.

Another time, Woody and his team found themselves at an apartment fire where thirteen units were burning. He heard a woman screaming that her baby was inside. "We raced in and stayed close to the wall. I did not see the baby but found a poodle that was still alive, so I broke a window outside the first floor and got the poodle safely on the ground. But I could not find the baby. The next thing I heard was one of our guys yelling, 'Hey Woody, we have the baby, and she is safe.' I was relieved and it turned out, that the poodle I got out was this woman's baby."

Firefighters are always walking on the edge of death. But thanks to their extensive training and teamwork, they believe the risk is worth it. "There are no lone wolves in the fire service. We watch each other's back and we become a band of brothers in the truest sense of the word," Woody explained. But even for this seasoned professional—who estimates he has fought thousands of fires in his career and seven fires during one day in a twenty-four-hour shift—danger is never far from his consciousness.

December 2004 was one fire that almost cost Woody his life. He and his partner, Michelle Smith, received a call at 10:45 a.m. where he was told that the owner of the home was out of town, but a daughter was possibly trapped on the second floor in her room. Since Michelle and Woody's Engine Company Fourteen were first on the scene, they needed to go into the burning house right away despite no other engines being present. "We did not see any fire, just smoke, so I put my hand against the door which was extremely hot," Woody recalled. "I opened the door and stayed low to the ground and after two minutes nothing happened. I tried to find a wedge to keep the door open. But I could not find one," Woody recalled. Two minutes later an explosion blew down the hall and the door slammed shut. "I could hear the fire rolling behind the door and it blew my mask off, and I was taking in smoke. I got my mask back on my face and then, I was told, I got Michelle out. That is the last thing I remembered," Woody recalled.

Woody does not remember much from that explosion except the chilling words he heard the paramedics say when they put him in the ambulance. "His blood pressure is 60/40 and we are losing him," he heard the paramedic's say as they started CPR. "I did not feel anything. *I am dying; this is it,* I thought. But I was not upset. I was ready."

Woody woke up in the hospital the next morning struggling to breathe. He suffered major lung damage and other injuries requiring him to be out of work for eight months and to be hooked up to breathing machines. His rehabilitation took one year, and he did try to return to the fire department but was not doing very well. To make matters worse, during one seizure call, his partner was trying to calm a man by holding him down. She placed a bite stick in his mouth so he would not swallow his tongue, and when he came to, he was disoriented and punched Woody's partner. Woody saw the attack and rushed to his partner's aid, jumping on the man to prevent him from lashing out again. Woody's shoulder hit the pavement hard, and he was in excruciating pain, especially since he had just had surgery a couple of months before the incident. Woody knew his firefighting days were over. In 2007, Woody hung up his hat and firefighting gear and was done.

But even though he suffered serious injuries, there were triumphs that Woody and his fellow firefighters would always remember fondly. During the terrorist attacks on 9/11, Woody was returning from a fire call and filling out his report. He heard that a plane hit a building but did not think that much of it. When the second plane hit the South Tower of the World Trade Center, he realized the enormity of the attack and went into firefighter mode.

He learned that 343 firefighters and one New York fire patrolman were lost that horrific day and asked if he could be the North Carolina liaison to assist in the rescue and recovery efforts. The North Carolina fire marshal, Jim Long, agreed, and Woody headed to Ground Zero to lend his assistance. "First, I went by myself and later with four fifteen-passenger vans to help transport the families of the fallen firefighters back and forth to Ground Zero. We had eight of us from the Fire Marshal's Office traveling to lower Manhattan. Charley Williams was the New York City battalion chief and the person who was in charge of Ground Zero. As bodies were pulled from the burning rubble, we could see they still had their names visible on their jackets," Woody recalled. "As the families came to identify their loved ones, we stood as an honor guard on the ramp to pay our respects and give them a proper send off, as we would for our own," Woody said.

On September 15, three thousand people attended the funeral Mass at St. Francis of Assis for Father Mychal Judge, the chaplain to the New York Fire Department. He was the first casualty of 9/11. President Bill Clinton and Hillary Clinton were among the mourners. Woody and the North Carolina chaplain, Gene Moore, were asked to attend the memorial and Father Patrick asked if they would say a few words. As they walked in, church cameras were everywhere. "I was honored to be part of the tribute and this is what I said: 'Our hearts are with all of the victims including Father Judge. He would be proud to know that all of the fire service members from across the country are unified in our love and support. That is why we are here.'"

After returning from Ground Zero, Woody, along with his fellow North Carolina firefighters, raised more than $7 million to support the families of the fallen firefighters who lost their lives that fateful day in New York City. In 1999, Woody had also been planning a local Fallen Firefighter's Memorial in North Carolina, but money was always a challenge. But after 9/11, the memorial's fundraising skyrocketed. On May 6, 2006, the Fallen Firefighter's Memorial was officially dedicated and is located in Raleigh right across from Central Fire Station Number One.

* * *

Still, Elvis was ever present in Woody's life. Over the years, he would take his show to entertain wounded warriors at the old Walter Reed in Washington, DC and bring gifts and much needed items for men and women severely injured in the War on Terror. There was one particular Christmas party that Woody remembers and which still brings tears to his eyes. "I was at the Malone House where families of patients stay while their sons or daughters are in the hospital, and I was helping the kids make their decorations," Woody recalled. "I was helping some of the kids create little angels and stars with glue guns, when one of the Army officers asked me if I could also sing for the kids. I had just finished my show at the hospital and thought, *why not?*"

Woody sang three or four Elvis songs that he thought the kids might enjoy like "Blue Christmas," "White Christmas," and "Silver Bells." After he finished, a little redheaded five-year-old girl with no front teeth and wearing a red reindeer nose walked toward the front of the room. "This child was so cute and came right up to me and hugged my leg. I was so touched. Then she said, 'Mr. Elvis, I love your Christmas music, can you sing some more?' Of course, I obliged," Woody recalled.

At the party, Woody talked to the child's mother, who told him her father, an injured soldier, was in surgery and that was why he was not at the party. The little girl continued to make some other decorations and Woody complimented the snow man she had made and placed on the Christmas tree. "Mr. Elvis, I made this just for you," she said.

"I lost it," said Woody. "There was hardly a dry eye in the room."

After Woody's first trip, he asked some of the Walter Reed officials and wounded warriors with whom he'd become friendly what items they needed. They gave him a lengthy list of things such as bibles, chocolate, diapers, shaving cream, paper and pencils, books, CDs, gift cards, and a wide range of groceries. Woody was on the case. "I drove to Walter Reed three times a week from North Carolina, which was about 227 miles away. We collected so many items that the Malone House put them in their storage area so the wounded warriors and their families could stop by anytime and pick out what they needed," Woody said. After a year, Woody delivered more gift cards from Target and Walmart and continued to send 150 fruit baskets and toys for the kids every Christmas as well as performing his annual Elvis Christmas show.

And as Woody's Elvis show began to reach even wider audiences and receive rave reviews, he was asked to perform for the troops in Afghanistan. He joined the Washington Redskins cheerleaders for a choreographed performance where the cheerleaders danced to Woody's playlist of the most popular Elvis songs. In February 2005, the group performed fourteen shows in two weeks. Woody was in his glory.

When Walter Reed Army Medical Center merged with the National Naval Medical Center in 2011, the Walter Reed National Military Medical Center was created. Today it provides world class healthcare to our nation's fighting forces as well as retirees and their families.

At the new location, Woody took his show to the "Warrior Café"—the cafeteria that served food and beverages to wounded warriors living in outpatient apartments in Building 62. His Elvis Christmas party tradition continued. Now in its twentieth year, it has become one of the time-honored holiday traditions at Walter Reed and a source of joy and laughter for the most severely injured military members and their families.

In retirement from his firefighting days, Woody immersed himself into doing everything he could to help wounded warriors and first responders. The experience at Walter Reed, as well as getting to know and working with Gary Sinise—who created the Gary Sinise Foundation to provide services to military members and their families, as well as veterans and first responders—touched him deeply. Gary also asked Woody to open for him during some of his Lt. Dan Band Concerts, and to perform at Invincible Spirit Festivals that Gary hosted at military bases across the country. Woody also became good friends with another dedicated and enthusiastic volunteer—Jennifer Griffin—FOX News national security correspondent, who also volunteered at Walter Reed with her three children, as well as many other events where she would be a co-host or emcee.

A former FOX News host, Bill O'Reilly, helped to promote the Independence Fund, with which Woody, Jennifer, and Gary would also be involved. The goal of the Fund was to provide money for special track chairs that severely wounded warriors could use in place of wheelchairs to give them the freedom to go where they could not maneuver before, including rough terrain, wooded areas, and even beaches. The average cost of the customized track chair was $15,000. Today more than 1,500 have been delivered at no charge to wounded warriors across the country.

But Woody's most recent project, and something he is most proud of, began at a Palm Key, Florida retreat hosted by the Gary Sinise Foundation. It was there that fifty veterans came together to relax, talk about their feelings, and enjoy the outdoors. "When we were at the campfires, we talked about everything and I could see the healing take place," Woody said. "Man, I thought it would be amazing to do something similar year-round. A place where wounded warriors could relax, take classes, and share the experience with other warriors. Gary's weekend inspired me to build my own camp that I called *Camp for Heroes*—so I did." Woody added.

Woody said that Gary has inspired so many people to get involved helping wounded warriors, first responders, gold star mothers, and families of the fallen. "Being who Gary is and what he is about has inspired me, and as a result, I knew what I needed to do," said Woody.

Woody was always a decent artist, and now in retirement, he had more time to focus on his creative side. He painted a lively collage depicting Gary Sinise leading the Lt. Dan Band. In May 2015, during Fleet Week in New York City, there was a fundraising event held at the Hard Rock Café, where

Woody and Jennifer were the emcees. Woody convinced Gary to allow him to auction the painting off, with half of the funds going to the Gary Sinise Foundation and the other half to the Independence Fund's arts programs. Woody was hoping he could also use the experience to raise money for his camp idea.

Bill O'Reilly and Gary Sinise both signed the painting. It sold for a whopping $100,000!

The gentleman who bought the painting was a Texas philanthropist who was so impressed with Woody that he asked him how he could help. "I told him we need a camp," Woody said.

"What do you need exactly?" the man asked.

"Well, I have the property, but I will need at least $450,000 to close the deal and build the camp," Woody told him.

"How about if I give you $50,000 for now and we can ask the property owners if they would give us six months more to raise the money to pay it off?" the man responded.

Woody was thrilled, but knew he needed even more money to make his camp a reality. Fortunately, at least for Woody, because the Independence Fund eliminated its arts program, they sent him a refund check of $50,000. "I was ecstatic," said Woody. "I had enough money to convince the owners if I gave them $100,000, they would close on the property in three months; they agreed. Then, to my surprise, the Texas philanthropist offered a tricked-up Ford truck for me to raffle. But it only raised $70,000, so I was still short $280,000," said Woody.

Soon Woody's luck would change, and as he explained, "God works in mysterious ways." Woody's attorney could not believe it was possible for Woody to only have three months to raise the extra funds. And he said so during a meeting the pair had in his office. Then, to Woody's astonishment, he received a call from his attorney soon after he left the meeting. During an event at Walter Reed that same day, his attorney called him and said: "Woody, your Texas benefactor just wired me the $280,000 you need to build the camp; it is entirely paid for."

"I bawled my eyes out," said Woody. "I could not believe this man's generosity. I decided I would pay him back every penny and wanted to show my appreciation but was not sure how. But I could not reach him after. I must have made over twenty phone calls, emails, and text messages. So, I had an idea. I received an incredibly special knife—one of only three ever produced. It was a made with the steel from the World Trade Center debris. It was a gift to thank me for helping after 9/11 at Ground Zero, and I decided to give it to him," Woody explained.

Finally, Woody was able to reach his benefactor, and Woody told him about the knife and that he wanted him to have it. The man was excited, and Woody asked him if he wanted him to come to Texas or if he wanted to receive the knife in New York City. His benefactor said he would love to come to New York and so Woody set the plan in motion.

The first part of the event was a ride on a New York City Fireboat with a close up view of the Statue of Liberty. Then for the official presentation Woody took the benefactor and his wife to an Italian restaurant—one of Gary's favorites—where Woody made sure he sat right next to the man whose generosity he could still not comprehend. "I got you where I want you," Woody said. "I am going to pay you back; I do not want you to worry; I am good for it," said Woody.

The benefactor placed his hand on Woody's shoulder and said, "My friend, your debt is paid with me." Woody could not believe his good fortune and the angel on his shoulder.

Woody still was hoping to raise more money from the truck raffle and told his benefactor that he would repay him once the truck was sold. "I know we have three more months for the raffle of the truck that you donated to us so I will give the money back to you when it is over," Woody said. "No, Woody, I want you to keep the money because I know you will need tractors on the farm, and I am sure many other things to get the camp up and running." Woody gave him the hug of all hugs.

"Nothing is impossible with God by your side," Woody said. And that is how *Camp for Heroes* was born. Five years later, more than 750 wounded warrior first responders have spent time together in a bucolic setting, learning how to live life again with joy and hope.

What makes a man such as Woody risk his life fighting fires, dress up and perform Elvis songs, auction paintings for charity, and build a camp for the heroes he loves and admires? "When I see people hopeless and helpless, [and] then see them triumph, I am happy. All of a sudden, they feel hope again," said Woody. "I am not going to lie; I took it hard when I lost a family of six in a house fire. It was a tough one. But if I had not showed up to console the other family members and friends, it would have been much worse. Though I have faced death myself and had serious injuries, I would do it all over again. It was my job and what I signed up to do," Woody explained.

Woody said that being a firefighter comes with risk but that good training prepares the person for every eventuality. "I guess you could say we are a special breed. Without our help, innocent people could perish, but because of our rescue and firefighting training, we have more saves than losses. I think a true firefighter has an overwhelming desire to make a difference and always pushes forward. You have to be a little bit crazy to do the things others would not do. My police officer friends always ask me how I could run into a burning building. And I would ask them back, how they can enter a building or stop a vehicle and get shot? It is who we are and how we are made, and I would do it all over again knowing I helped make the world a better place," Woody said.

Twelve

THE FIREBRAND

Each time a woman stands up for herself, she stands up for all women.
—Maya Angelou

I F IT WERE UP TO NICOLE SCOTT, YOUNG GIRLS GROWING UP TODAY WOULD dream about becoming firefighters. They would not hesitate. They would instinctively realize that there are no jobs that men can do better than women, and that being vulnerable is a sign of strength, not weakness. Nicole has been both a trailblazer and healer. She is a firefighter and firebrand.

Nicole was born in Louisiana but has lived in Napa Valley, California for most of her life. She has two biological sisters, and four stepsisters. Her parents divorced when she was in the sixth grade, which made things difficult for a young girl longing for stability and acceptance.

Despite being surrounded by her sisters and stepsisters who wore makeup and relished being cheerleaders, Nicole was the consummate tomboy. "I loved playing tackle football and never wanted a Barbie doll. I disliked wearing anything that would even resemble a dress," said Nicole. "I was into playing with my GI Joe, and the only way I would take off my football jersey is when my parents would force me to put on a dress for church; I was not having it," she recalled.

Nicole loved sports and played t-ball, softball, volleyball, and basketball. They were her life and made her feel a sense of belonging and accomplishment. She was so talented in softball that she played for her college team at Chico State University.

"My dad was an engineer and was happier reading the *Wall Street Journal* than watching a Sunday Night Football game on television. Luckily, my stepdad was into sports and like me he looked up to athletes as role models," Nicole recalled. "Back then there was never a female firefighter or police officer that any of us would think of as a role model, so as I got older, my career goals were fairly limited," said Nicole.

As Nicole continued to play sports in college, she decided she wanted to become a teacher, coach, or athletic trainer. "When I was in the eighth grade, I thought I wanted to become a nurse so I could be around people and help them. I was fortunate in college to become an athletic trainer and decided to throw my hat in the ring to work with the football team," said Nicole. She would put her interest in nursing on the back burner.

Nicole and three other women eventually became athletic trainers for the football team. "It was awesome," said Nicole. "I think the guys were caught off guard, but we got along well. It was then that I fell in love with training and especially helping to rehab the football players when they were injured," said Nicole.

The three women trainers went to every practice and were there during and after every game. They volunteered their time and that experience solidified Nicole's dream of getting involved in some type of helping profession. After her college graduation in 1998, Nicole soon realized that there were absolutely no jobs for women athletic trainers, so she moved in with her mother and stepfather to try and save money and figure out what career she wanted to pursue.

Rather than slipping into despair because her dream of being a trainer was dashed, Nicole pushed on and got a job at the Queen of the Valley Hospital, a position that she did not realize would alter the trajectory of her life.

She was essentially a cafeteria worker. "I was setting up the cafeteria for morning and lunch meetings and I felt like a caterer," Nicole remembered. "I also would have to restock the nursing station with crackers, cookies, and drinks, and I would catch myself standing in the emergency room watching all the excitement. I was especially intrigued by the x-rays that I saw hanging in the doctor's office in the emergency room and tried to figure out what I was looking at."

Nicole applied and was accepted to EMT school. When she graduated, she was hired by the Queen of the Valley Hospital as an emergency room technician. It was there that she got to know a number of the firefight-ers and ambulance crews as they brought patients to the emergency room. "Wow, this looks exciting, and I realized that maybe becoming an EMT would be fun and something I could be happy doing every day," Nicole said. "Working in the Emergency Room is what drove me to want to work on an ambulance and that's when I applied to do just that," she added.

Nicole applied and was hired by the Piners Ambulance Company where she worked from 2000–2003. Since the hospital where she worked before was a trauma center, she witnessed numerous accidents with victims who were flown in from across the county. "In Napa we would run calls with the fire guys, and I found them to be among the most caring and compassion-ate guys I ever met," said Nicole. "Over time one of the guys I knew on the engine company asked me, 'Why don't you consider being a firefighter? You should apply.' I was flattered but I literally knew nothing about firefighting and was very green; plus I had no idea of what the firefighter culture was like."

While contemplating what being a firefighter would entail, especially being a woman, Nicole decided to further her body of knowledge by apply-ing to paramedic school. While working full time at Piners Ambulance, Nicole attended paramedic school. She also applied and was accepted to the Napa City Fire Reserve Program, where she attended training sessions twice a month. That decision would also be a groundbreaking one for Nicole.

Nicole learned that the Novato Fire District was hiring. That was the good news. The unwelcome news was that no women ever made it through the academy or were hired for full-time firefighter positions, though some women were part of the reserve program at Novato Fire Protection District. And the process for employment was grueling. "In order to get hired, you have to go through an interview process, do a medical scenario, pass a physi-cal agility test and medical exam, and a background check," said Nicole. "Once you pass all of this, they will offer you a job. Then you must go to the academy for about sixteen weeks, and after you pass, only then can you go to the floor and work as a full-time firefighter," Nicole added.

She also learned that full-time firefighters work forty-eight hours on and ninety-six hours off, and Nicole was pumped. This was the beginning of a firefighting career that would span twenty years, have its share of challenges and triumphs, and launch her into another phase of the profession that would save lives and souls.

"Me and two other women were the first three women ever who gradu-ated from the academy and became full-time firefighters. It was awesome, but we soon realized there would be some challenges; growing pains actu-ally," said Nicole. "The guys were great, but in Novato they never dealt with women in the fire station. I think it took a number of months before we all got used to each other," she added.

Not only did they have to learn how to deal with women at the fire station, but there were structural issues that presented their own unique challenges. For example, bathrooms. In the past, they were designed just for men. That had to change. And bedrooms. Two of the male firefighters would share the same room with a divider in between. Surely, Nicole would not find that too appealing. Those were the easy fixes.

There were other issues that took a bit more time to adjust, according to Nicole. "It was kind of funny," Nicole said. "When we would go on an everyday medical call, we would wear dark blue Nomex [fire resistant] pants and our blue t-shirts. When we would have to go to a grass fire, we would have to take our blue t-shirts off and put on a long sleeve t-shirt. Then we would put on a long sleeve jacket and put on yellow pants over our Nomex pants. Basically, we needed two layers of protection when we fight grass fires. So, when we would get a call, there was no time to change in the bath-room. But we did not care; we just took our shirts off. The looks on the guys' faces were priceless!"

Over time the male firefighters became used to Nicole and the other female firefighters wearing sports bras. "After all," she said, "It's just like wearing a bathing suit. I knew that early on the guys felt uncomfortable, and I could understand that, but over time it was not an issue. We were just one of the guys and we wanted to be treated the same."

Because Nicole was now a firefighter as well as a paramedic, she was as comfortable working on an engine as she was on an ambulance. "When we receive a 911 call the engine usually gets there first," said Nicole. "Many people ask us why an engine is normally there first and not an ambulance? I tell them that the firefighter on the engine is also a paramedic and they perform the patient assessment and then the ambulance arrives a minute later," Nicole added.

Nicole explained that on the ambulance there are two firefighters, who are also paramedics. It is their job to grab the gurney and bring it to where the patient is located before they transport the patient to the hospital. "People also ask us why the fire department is always there with an ambulance on a

911 call?" Nicole said. "It is an issue of manpower. If a person is in cardiac arrest, we have to do a lot of things at the scene that take a lot of hands. There are times when we have to lift a three-hundred-pound patient down a flight of stairs or cut a hole in the wall of a room to get a six-hundred-pound person out of their house."

During actual fires, Nicole is all in as a firefighter. She loves being able to help people during the most traumatic times in their lives, thinking little about her own safety. But over time she would discover that the job comes with a downside. According to the National Fallen Firefighter's Foundation, fire service members are at a higher risk of suicide than the general population.[1] "Among other factors, the nature of emergency response work and the exposure it brings, means that the majority of firefighters and EMS responders become an at-risk population from their first days on the job. They are at least four-times more likely to experience a suicide than a line-of-duty death," they reported. And the 2015 national study of a thousand firefighters by researchers from Florida State University (FSU) reveals "nearly half of the respondents say they had suicidal thoughts at one or more points in their firefighting career. Furthermore, approximately 15 percent reported one or more suicide attempts." In addition, Nicole explained that firefighters experience PTSD and depression five times higher than the civilian population.

Nicole recalls one of her many experiences that brings that point home. "There was one call where a gentlemen—who had multiple DUIs—was riding his motorcycle, went through a four way stop sign, and hit a father and his young daughter as they were crossing the street. I worked on the dad whose leg was crushed; his daughter suffered numerus traumatic injuries and we knew she would not make it. Tragically, she passed away the next day," Nicole said.

The injured father asked Nicole if his daughter was okay. He was bleeding profusely, and Nicole said while she always tries to be as honest as possible, it is a fine line to walk. "You have to be honest but at the same time take care of the patient you are treating. I tried to comfort the father by telling him, 'Sir, your daughter is with the other medics and is going to hospital. She is in critical condition, but she is in good hands.' It was very tough for

---

1   "Florida State University Study on Firefighter Suicide," National Fallen Firefighter's Foundation, September 9, 2015, https://wwwfirehero.org.

me and still is to some extent because I drive by that intersection all the time and I know that little girl died there."

Nicole has had her share of traffic fatalities over her career. Sadly, she has also witnessed numerous suicides—those who chose to hang themselves still give her nightmares.

"There was a lady in her sixties who was staying at a hotel," Nicole recalled. "We received a call with a possible 1055, meaning it was a dead person. I knew it was not going to be pretty. We went in her room and found the note she left. Then we saw our victim with the belt from her robe wrapped around her neck and somehow, she managed to get it up over the door. It was so sad because the lady never checked out and the hotel manager found her and was in tears. For me, since it was my first hanging, I thought the lady looked like she was sleeping. It was eerie because she did not look dead," Nicole added.

Another hanging that broke Nicole's heart was a high school student who hung himself from a tree. After they attended to the young man, they had to break the news to his parents. "It was extremely difficult," said Nicole. "My partner and I walked over to the parents. I put my hand on the father's back, looked him in the eye, and said, 'I am so sorry to tell you this but your son has died. There was nothing we could do. His heart stopped a long time ago, way before we got to him.' The parents started to cry, and they hugged each other. We realized they needed some space and that is when we left," Nicole recalled.

"Being a woman, the human touch comes more naturally to me so that is why I gently put my arm around the father and hugged him," Nicole said. "I always try to read the scene and determine if it is okay to put my arm around a parent or hug them. I can tell when people need a comforting touch."

During Nicole's nineteen years at Novato, she has been on thousands of calls. Shootings, suicides, overdoses, grass fires, structure fires, vehicle fires, and much more.

There was one call Nicole and her partner went on where someone put a rag in the garage that caught on fire and spread from the garage to the kitchen, and then throughout the house. "Me and my engine company were the first on the scene. We entered through the front door and the smoke was thick, and I could feel the flames over my head. Fortunately, everyone got out. There were four engines, a ladder truck, ambulance, and our battalion chief, who arrived in his own vehicle," Nicole explained.

It took about thirty minutes to get the fire under control, but the garage and kitchen were ruined. The family was watching their house go up in flames and was naturally traumatized. "We are always trying to help the family in cases like this," Nicole explained. "Our chief comes to the scene and runs the fire from the Fire Command Vehicle. Then another chief will come in a separate vehicle and will become the safety officer. When there is a structure fire, the majority of the time we will call in a fire investigator to the scene to rule out arson. The fire investigator will interview the witnesses and family members. Then the Red Cross will be called to take care of the families' needs including finding a hotel, providing food and clothing, and anything else they need to get back on their feet."

Nicole said that arson fire investigators are trained to assess whether a fire appears suspicious or not. For example, if there is a grass fire on the top of a hill where there is normally no foot traffic, or if in a structure fire there is a smell of an accelerant—those might be triggers of a possible arson.

Over the years at Novato, Nicole proved herself as a capable and exemplary firefighter. It was never a gender issue—with a few exceptions. "We laugh about it now, but there was a time when an older gentleman would say something to me like, 'Oh they let you drive?' or 'They let you put out fires, too?' I would be polite but would have to explain that we do the same job as the guys. And there was one time during a St. Patrick's Day Parade where we were all lined up wearing our uniforms when two men, also in uniform, shook every firefighter's hand but mine. I was surprised but not surprised," Nicole said.

That was back then; now things have changed. Nicole is just one of the guys and at forty-six, among the most beloved team members. "My department has the most loving and supportive guys I have ever met, and we all are like one big family," she said. "They know me, and I know them, and, luckily, they took me in and we learned to trust each other. We are part of each other's families, and we literally spend more time together than with our own."

Spending night and day with Nicole's firefighter colleagues bonded them emotionally. Nicole realized that after a tough call, for example, some of the guys would open up and confide in her about their emotions—a role she relished. She also realized that people cope in diverse ways and that many of her colleagues were struggling, especially when they would work long hours, then try to transition to family life. Or they would spend so much time away from home that they would miss cherished family activities. "In our male-dominated culture, it was not acceptable to talk about your feelings because it was a sign of weakness. I tried to be there for my guys and help them talk about things that were buried deep inside; I knew I could help," said Nicole.

One night as Nicole was sitting at the fire station, a police officer mentioned that he just returned from a peer support training and was wondering why he never saw any firefighters in attendance?

"When the officer came in and talked to me about the peer support program training, I told him that I never even heard of a peer support program. I asked him what it was. I learned all about it from him and knew we had to have that type of program here. I went to my chief and told him about it," said Nicole. "They had the insight and concern to address the problem head-on. We decided to start a peer support program not only for Novato Fire but also for our Marin Professional Firefighters: International Association of Fire Fighters (IAFF) Local 1775. It is now called the 'Marin County Peer Support Team,'" Nicole explained. Nicole said that IAFF surveyed seven thousand firefighters across North America. The results reported that 87 percent of those firefighters believe that the stigma of mental health creates a barrier for seeking help. And 81 percent are afraid to talk about their "emotional baggage" because they are worried that they will be seen as weak or unfit for duty.[2]

There was also a conference on suicide—Behavioral Health for Firefighters—planned in Sacramento in 2016; Nicole's chief asked her if she wanted to attend. "'Yes, for sure I want to go.' It really lit the fire in me, and I was anxious to attend the conference," Nicole recounted. "I got the support from our chiefs and everyone on the floor. I started working with our local 1775 vice president after the conference to start a peer support program for not only the Novato Fire District but for our Local 1775—The Marin County Peer Support Team. It was an eye-opening conference and I got to work with ten different fire departments in Marin County, which gave me a broad spectrum of the issues they face, and how to solve mental health challenges in the fire service in general."

After the conference, Nicole's chief said, "Hey, the State is opening a task force on mental health; do you want to be on it?"

"Damn straight I do," Nicole exclaimed.

2 "Supporting Fire Fighter Mental Health," International Association of Fire Fighters, https://iaff.org.

She was chosen to be on the task force in 2016. They discussed best practices for behavioral health for firefighters as well as implementing peer support policies and connections. Nicole's chief was ready for her to get started, and she was excited to put her knowledge to work and make it happen. "I can say all the chiefs and guys have supported the program one hundred percent. As a result, more guys would come to me and talk about their depression, anxiety, and suicidal ideation. I was also able to teach classes on meditation, yoga, and coping with PTSD," Nicole said. "I also attended a two-day International Association of Firefighters workshop that encompassed the entire country and would function as a bridge that connects our people to employee assistance services," Nicole said.

After taking the Peer Support Class, and with great enthusiasm knowing she would put it to effective use, Nicole became a certified peer support team member.

What is a certified peer support team member? "We have been trained in California to use our individual experiences as well as evidence-based practices to help people who struggle with mental health issues," Nicole explained. "We listen to our peers, ask them the tough questions, and support them with coping techniques and self-help strategies that we learned in the class," she added.

Nicole knows her firefighter peers so well that she can detect when one of them is hurting. In addition, after a particularly difficult run, she will arrange a meeting with the group of firefighters who participated in that call and bring them together to talk about their feelings. "There are five of us on my support team and we are all very close," Nicole said. "I make sure I text all the guys, especially after a bad call. We call this an 'Atypical Call Policy.' It is a valuable tool that we use that has really helped everyone 'defuse.'"

Nicole said that the Atypical Call Policy works like this: "When there are difficult calls such as pediatric calls, suicides, and fatal vehicle accidents, for example, the battalion chief on duty contacts a peer support team member. He or she gives them the details of the call and who was involved," Nicole explained. "Within a few hours after the call, the peer support team member will go to one of the stations and will meet with the firefighters who were on the call. No one is forced to attend the meetings, which is what defusing is all about. It is very informal and we just talk and process the call together for about thirty minutes."

"The peer support team member takes the pulse on how everyone is doing and feeling and will follow-up with these members a few days after defusing. Some firefighters are fine right after a call but sometimes it takes a few days for the call to hit them, and then they will want to talk," Nicole added.

One day, Nicole was working at the station when a call came in the late afternoon that was shocking. This was one of Nicole's hard calls, or as she and her colleagues refer to them, "the top ten terrible calls." While she did not respond to that call personally, she knew right away that the firefighters who did would need some help processing the incident.

"I was working on the engine when the call came down that a male subject lit himself on fire in the intersection of Redwood and DeLong Streets in Novato. When I read the reports, I knew it was going to be a horrible call for both the firefighters and police officers," Nicole said.

Nicole knew she had to intervene and initiate the Atypical Call Policy right away. "I called the Novato Police Peer Support Team leader and we talked and both agreed to have a defusing session forty-five minutes after the incident at Station 61. She contacted all of the police officers involved in the incident, and I did the same for my crew," Nicole said.

Once Nicole's crew was back in the "zone," meaning back in Novato, and the patient was brought to the emergency room, Nicole's battalion chief took the engine and medics out of service. Nicole raced to Station 61 and went upstairs to meet the police officers and firefighters for the confidential defusing session. All of the participants came voluntarily and the only people in the room were actually involved in the call, as well as Nicole and her team.

"Basically, what we do in these defusing sessions is go around the room and talk chronologically in the order of who was on scene and what happened. By processing the call together and hearing what the police and firefighters saw, puts all the pieces together like a jigsaw puzzle. By knowing the sequence of events, there is no discrepancy and it is easier for the mind to process," Nicole explained.

Nicole said that while everything in the defusing sessions is confidential, there is a quantifiable process she follows as a trained peer support leader. "Once we go around the room and identify the issues that all of the people on the call experienced, I tell them to take care of themselves. That means both physically and emotionally. I want them to recognize the signs and symptoms of PTSD, suicidal ideation, anxiety, and depression. When it is all said and done, I hope they will feel better and less stressed and know what to do in case they experience any resulting mental health issues," said

Nicole. "For first responders, when the auto pilot shuts off, that is when emotions can become raw and confusing. We all can relate to what a small burn feels like and the resulting pain, but in the case of the man who lit himself on fire that is extremely sad and makes the situation even worse for our first responders. The good news is that we have programs to help, unlike in the past."

Nicole had another situation where a firefighter returned home after a bad call and decided to take some time off. "I kept in touch with him almost every day because I could sense he was in pain. There was one day when we spoke that he mentioned he was feeling suicidal. I said to him, 'Alright, can we talk? I know you are having a tough time, and I am going to get you some help.' I also talked to his wife. We then made a date to get together. I realized he was suffering from severe PTSD, and I was able to get him the help he needed," Nicole said.

Nicole also shared a disturbing 2018 survey where it was reported that firefighter suicides exceeded the rate of on-duty deaths by about 30 percent on average. Eighteen out of every hundred thousand firefighters' deaths are by suicide compared to thirteen for every hundred thousand of the general population. Because of the stigma associated with mental health issues, four to five thousand or 80 percent of the respondents did not ask for help because of that stigma. "I have seen many guys believing that if they talk about their issues, that is seen as weakness," Nicole said. "Eventually, something will explode because of that fear and keeping those destructive feelings buried inside. That can result in excessive drinking, sleep deprivation, and depression, and all of those are linked to suicide calls. My goal is to mitigate and alleviate the fear and never have another firefighter suffer in silence," she added.

Nicole also attended a retreat in Northern California called the West Coast Trauma Retreat. It is designed for first responders who are experiencing PTSD, anxiety, and depression. There is a six-month waiting list, but Nicole was chosen to lend her expertise.. "I honestly believe that being a woman lessens the blow and helps people calm down, both the firefighter and the victim. This is especially true when dealing with rape victims, for example, who are more comfortable talking to a woman. My peer support training is helpful in these situations as well, giving me the skills to know how to manage victims suffering from unspeakable violence."

Nicole said there have been times when her male counterparts, in situations such as a woman going into labor, will tell Nicole when she arrives on the scene, "Thank God you are here."

As one of the first women firefighters and trailblazers, Nicole has some advice for girls growing up today who might consider firefighting as a career. "I was among the first women in a role that was male dominated. I may not be as physically strong as the guys, but I can do the same job as they can and so can you. You can be what you want to be. You can do this, and do not let society tell you anything different. And when you are older like me, you will care less about what people think. Most of all, you will be open to taking care of your mental health and those you love. As the great Olympic gold medalist Michael Phelps said in one of his commercials, 'Therapy for all.'"

While never a braggadocio, Nicole said she was "shocked" to receive the coveted EMS Cross Award. She was unaware that her friend nominated her for this prestigious award that recognizes a uniformed EMT who by act and deed represents the most outstanding achievement or accomplishment in EMS over an extended period. It also is the highest award that can be conferred in the absence of extreme conditions and extraordinary circumstances, according to the award criteria. "Earlier this year I was totally shocked when I learned I was going to receive the EMS Cross Award. Like so many of my colleagues, we do what we do because we care, not because of the recognition we might receive. The thanks we get from the people we help every day is enough for me," Nicole said.

Nicole is committed to breaking down walls, not burning down the house. Her advocacy for the mental health of fellow firefighters is unrelenting. So much so that after she retires from firefighting, she hopes to take on an even bigger challenge.

"My goal in the future is to stay in the mental health field. I am committed to continue working with first responders and receiving my life coach certification in trauma. For all the young women out there, I hope you will never give up on your dreams and think out of the box. When I changed my career goal from being a teacher and coach to a firefighter, it was the best decision I have ever made," said Nicole.

Thirteen

THE AX WITH AN AXE

Nothing is so strong as gentleness, nothing so gentle as real strength.
—Saint Francis de Sales

A T SIX FOOT TWO AND 240 POUNDS, JIMMY AXIOTIS COULD WRESTLE
even the most fit of his teammates. You could say he was a physical
goliath. As a high school athlete and a member of his wrestling and
football teams, Jimmy was a force to contend with. Not only did he tower
over most of his classmates, but he excelled in every sport he pursued. He
even considered becoming a professional athlete but his social life became
more of a priority and partying his vocation. But Jimmy had a distinctly
different side—this tough guy had a soft spot. A need to serve and help his
community. Where that would lead him as a young man he would not discover until a failed exam changed his world and future career.

Jimmy Axiotis was born on June 3, 1985, in Springfield, Massachusetts.
He was one of three boys—his brothers were named Mikey and Joey.
Jimmy was the youngest of the Axiotis clan. They lived in a tough neighborhood where the boys were exposed to gangs and way more drugs than
Jimmy's parents could tolerate. During their childhood years in Springfield,
Mikey was getting into trouble, primarily experimenting with drugs, much
to his parents' dismay. The only solution Jimmy's parents could agree on
was that they needed to move. "Mikey grew up in not the best atmosphere
and was getting in trouble a lot," Jimmy said. "He was getting more and
more involved in drugs and, when he was just thirty-nine, he was found

lying in an alley next to a drug house. He apparently died of a drug overdose," Jimmy added.

"This was one of the most trying times of my life since I worked in a field that saved many lives from drug overdoses. But I was not there to save my brother," Jimmy said. "To this day, I still struggle with his death and the tragic way he died. When he was clean and sober he was the best brother anyone could ever have, but when he was on drugs, he was a totally different person. I try to remember everything he taught me as a big brother, but I cannot help but think about him every time I deal with an overdose at work."

When Jimmy was ten years old, the family moved to Port Orange Florida. It is a small city in Volusia County and is part of the Deltona-Daytona Beach-Ormond Beach metropolitan area. Jimmy lived most of his life in Port Orange. But because he was a gifted athlete, and the local high school did not have a wrestling team, he received a variance and attended Atlantic High School in South Daytona Beach. He was a standout on both the wrestling and football teams. "I did not take my sports as seriously as a teenager," Jimmy recalled. "I loved to party and go out with my friends. I regret that I did not focus on my sports because I might have been able to receive a college scholarship," he added.

Still, Jimmy excelled in athletics and credits them for providing him with a solid foundation for the future. "I would say that sports gave me structure and set me up on a course that would lead me to where I am now. I had a good foundation and work ethic because of all my training, and though I did not recognize that when I was young, I sure do now," Jimmy added. It was no surprise that Jimmy's favorite subject in high school was physical education; he also had an aptitude for math. "I was always good with numbers and could work out problems in my head—even better than I could on paper. I did very well in all of my math subjects but was terrible in English. Thank goodness for spell check on my cell phone," he added.

Since playing professional sports was a pipe dream, Jimmy began to consider what he wanted to do in the future. "I always wanted to be a cop, said Jimmy. "I knew I could handle the physical challenges, and I also had a desire to help people and get the bad guys off the streets. I saw what being around those types of people did to my brother, and I wanted to make sure that would not happen to any other young person," he added.

Jimmy applied and was accepted into the Daytona State Police Academy. He did very well and received the Academy's coveted Top Gun

Award, and graduated at the top of his class. But when it came time to take the exam—which was the final step to becoming a certified police officer—Jimmy hit a roadblock. "I was still very young, but I was also very busy partying, and so, I did not study for the state exam the way I should have," Jimmy explained. "My partying took its toll and I did not pass. It was disappointing for sure, but I licked my wounds and got a job in construction. After doing that for a bit, I realized it was not for me and had to make another huge decision."

Jimmy realized he did not want to do construction work for the rest of his life and talked to one of his friends about his dilemma. "I was talking to a few buddies who were in fire school, and they told me how much they were into it and encouraged me to apply," Jimmy said. "I jumped at the chance and applied as soon as I could. I learned that firefighters typically work twenty-four hours straight and then forty-eight hours off and that sounded right up my alley. They all said how much they enjoyed the camaraderie and being with their crew. Most of all, they told me how good it felt knowing you are helping people and saving lives. That solidified my decision to become a firefighter," Jimmy added.

Jimmy always enjoyed helping people. "I always go out of my way to help people, sometimes more than I should. I guess you could say I am a 'people pleaser.' So, actually the idea of becoming a firefighter really suits my personality as well as my desire to serve," he added.

In 2008, Jimmy attended the Daytona State Fire School. The classes averaged about four months of intense training; then as part of the requirements, Jimmy also needed to take additional courses for approximately one more year to become a certified emergency medical technician (EMT). "It was a very tough course both mentally and physically," said Jimmy. "Since I played basketball and football I did very well on the physical aspects of firefighter training and usually shined. And being so tall, I was able to use my athletic side to my advantage. For example, when you have to carry your gear into a burning building—which we did practice in class—being more athletic and stronger really helps and can save your life as well as your squad, not to mention the victims of fires," he added.

Jimmy did well in fire school and also in EMT training. When he graduated in 2009, he was excited to begin a new career path and become one of the nation's first responders.

Jimmy sent in applications to several Florida fire departments as well as some that were out of state but after six months, was surprised that there were no job offers forthcoming. "I was applying everywhere but there were no jobs back then. I also noticed that, of the jobs I did see and wanted to apply for, all required the applicant to also be a paramedic," Jimmy recalled. He realized that having the paramedic certification would make him a higher quality candidate and more of an asset to the fire department. "Once I realized that, I jumped into paramedic school. Let me say it was one of the hardest classes I have ever taken academically. We had to learn everything about anatomy, physiology, drugs, and all the possible medical issues we would face as paramedics working in the fire department. Fortunately, I loved every minute and did very well."

After three semesters, voluminous amounts of paperwork, numerous books read, and hours of studying, Jimmy was on his way to becoming a certified paramedic; he was also among the top students in his class. "Once I was almost finished paramedic school, the first thing I did was to update all my applications, believing someone would call me back," Jimmy said. "I was shocked that I got a call almost immediately from Daytona for a job, but I had two more semesters to go. They agreed to keep me on probation at the fire department, knowing I was almost finished with school. It was a crazy but exhilarating time for me. I would be in class studying one day, working twenty-four hours the next, and then doing a clinical the following day. I did not have a day off for a month."

At twenty-four, Jimmy felt he had achieved his goal and felt a sense of accomplishment. "I found a great career path and never had anything like that before," Jimmy said. "Now I will have job security, great benefits, and that comfortable feeling that I did something well and succeeded," Jimmy added.

Jimmy graduated from paramedic school in 2010 and began working full time at the fire department. Since he was always a big, athletic guy, Jimmy believed it helped him being the new kid on the block. "It is always somewhat uncomfortable when anyone starts a new job, but I felt my size played to my advantage," Jimmy said. "When I first walked in, I realized that I did not get as much slack from the guys as they normally give out. Guys are guys, and they can always sense a weakling, and if they can get over you, they will. But it is all in good fun and part of our culture," Jimmy added.

Jimmy realized he had much to learn from his fellow firefighters and did everything he could to seek out their knowledge and practical experience. After all, being a firefighter is a dangerous and challenging job, and there was still much to absorb. "You have to tackle many physical challenges in firefighting, and we had practice sessions to help newbies like me know exactly what to do," said Jimmy. "Things such as pulling a charged hose line, running upstairs with a high-rise pack, hoisting hoses up buildings, using an axe to cut through a window, or dragging a dummy out of a simulated burning building. And you had to achieve those goals in a certain timeframe," Jimmy explained.

"When we practiced on test dummies, we had to drag them a certain number of yards. It is amazing how tired your legs become but you knew that you had to persevere to save that last person," said Jimmy.

To his colleagues, Jimmy was an impressive rookie. During the dummy test, he had the fastest times—averaging about three minutes to complete the test; the average was five to six minutes. It is the most important of the tests because, as Jimmy explained, "If you do not finish, they do not let you in, believing you are not ready to be a firefighter."

Jimmy was excited to be on the scene for his first structure fire but hoped his lack of experience would not be obvious and not affect the outcome of the rescue.

"I was super nervous walking in my first structure fire and not confident about what to expect," said Jimmy. "Everyone manages things differently and I knew I had a lot of knowledge to learn about fighting fires and removing people from accidents. But my inexperience sure made me nervous," he added.

As time went by, Jimmy found his sea legs. He worked tirelessly to apply his extensive training as a firefighter, EMT, and paramedic to his real-world experiences. "I soon realized that I had to rely on my training, especially for difficult cases such as a pediatric drowning or any other incident involving a child. I think all of my firefighter brothers and sisters as well as all first responders would agree," Jimmy explained.

In fact, it was not that long after his graduation that Jimmy did encounter his first tragedy involving a child. "When a pediatric drowning call goes out, we cannot panic and, though we are super nervous, that is when our training is put to the test," Jimmy recalled.

Jimmy remembers arriving at the scene where a six-year-old child was missing and found at the bottom of her family's swimming pool. The pool was filled with debris and algae, and it was obvious that it was not properly maintained. The parents were at work when the child fell in the pool; she was being cared for that day by a babysitter. "I was not the lead paramedic on call. I was scared and very nervous. It all seemed like a blur, and

I remember thinking, *what role do I play here?* I quickly jumped into action, holding my emotions inside as I assisted the medic with an IV, monitoring the child's cardiac rhythm, and assisting with rotating compressions," Jimmy recalled.

Apparently, the babysitter said the child wandered out to the pool on her own, but Jimmy and the team found that perplexing. When the parents arrived, they were screaming and, as more family members arrived, Jimmy could feel their anguish and pain. But he had a job to do and the goal was to transport the child to the hospital or, as Jimmy said, "load and go."

Jimmy rode along with the ambulance to the hospital. "We ride along with the ambulance to have some extra hands. Either they beat us, or we get there before them, but regardless, the more hands the better," Jimmy explained. "In this case, the police officer was also with us at the scene, which happens frequently. He brought the family members to a separate location away from the pool because he did not want them to see their child in this horrific condition. This one really hurt. I did not have a kid at the time, but I had a little niece and nephew and all I could picture was that happening to them," Jimmy explained. "It was so painful."

After bad calls like the drowning of a child, or a fire where people lost their lives, Jimmy said that a chaplain arrives and talks to the firefighters involved in the call and encourages them to express their feelings. "After bad calls like this one, the chaplain comes to the station for a de-briefing session and encourages us not to bottle things up. I tend to hold in my feelings the same way my dad did and do not talk about my feelings that much. But I do have support systems like my wife, Holly, and of course my colleagues, so that really helps," Jimmy said.

Jimmy also said that after tough calls, he tends to review the situation, research what could have been done better, and then put that knowledge to work for the next bad call. And there would be thousands in Jimmy's twelve-year career as a firefighter and paramedic.

"I always do my homework and as much research as I can to learn what should be done. What could I have done better? As a team we review the call and talk about what we did do right and what we could do even better. These after-action sessions help us continue our best practices and reinforce our training," Jimmy explained. But despite the efforts to become better professionals and the endless training, when children are involved, it is difficult to calm down, but it is mandatory to prevent the situation from becoming even more tragic.

"When kids are involved, you must calm down and resort to your training. In the case of that little girl who drowned in the pool, if we are on edge rushing to get things done, even the best firefighters can fumble. You cannot be all disheveled; you have to be calm and have a clear head," Jimmy said.

For example, Jimmy said that paramedics need to have their hands steady when they are inserting an IV in a patient in a moving vehicle. "My hands have to be steady, and I have to put my emotions on hold to be able to focus on my victim. I take a breath, then a second to realize I am there to help, not just rush in super-fast. I always look at the bigger picture," Jimmy added.

Jimmy has developed a thick skin over the years, though cases such as the little girl's drowning affect him from time to time. "After she passed away, she crossed my mind a lot. While I did not lose that much sleep, she was always on my mind for quite a while. And when I would hear a call go out, I would hope it was not a pediatric call," he added.

Another incident that profoundly affected Jimmy occurred in 2019. "I had a day off and I was going to the gym as I always do every morning. As I was working out, I happened to notice a small crowd gathering around the weight area. I walked over to see what was going on and saw a man lying on the ground and in obvious distress," said Jimmy. "I could not believe I actually knew the guy. His name was Sean, and he was a police officer for Daytona Beach. As I bent down to check him out, I saw his face was turning purple, which meant he was not breathing very well. I directed one of the guys to call 911. Sean became unconscious and had no pulse. I was zoned in on helping him. I started CPR immediately and told another guy to grab the AED [Automated External Defibrillator]. When he returned with the AED, I applied the pads to Sean's chest and let the device analyze his rhythm. It provided a shock to his heart. I continued CPR after the shock and was happy that he was trying to breathe on his own. That is when I stopped CPR and, thankfully, Sean finally had a pulse; what a relief," Jimmy recalled.

Once the ambulance and fire department arrived, they took over and Sean was transported to the hospital. "After that happened I was emotionally drained and did not continue my workout. I headed back home. On the way I called Holly and that is when it really hit me that I possibly saved my colleague's life," Jimmy recalled.

About a week later, and after Sean had recovered, he called Jimmy and told him, "Jimmy, I do not know what to say but thanks to you I can go home to my kids every day." Jimmy was touched by Sean's words.

"I felt that I really did something special that day, and all my training came into play for the best outcome possible," Jimmy said.

Being a member of a firefighting team has been among the most rewarding experiences for Jimmy. His colleagues have become just like family, and he feels fulfilled every day on the job. "I found my own spot and am comfortable in day-to-day in the operations of the fire department. We are full of different personalities. It is not always easy spending twenty-four hours a day with your crew. But they are truly your second family, and when you spend one third of your life with them, you learn how valuable those relationships are," Jimmy said. "Generally, we firefighters are a tight knit bunch, but there are times when someone wants to transfer to another station, and it is what it is. I am easy going, and I do not let people affect me much and I am not concerned what people think of me. I basically get along with everybody, and these men and women I work with hold a special place in my life."

One of the chiefs that has had a great influence on Jimmy and was his mentor was Chief Tyrell. "Chief Tyrell was the chief at my station in the early years. He had incredible knowledge and was also our long-time union president," Jimmy said. "Every time he would talk, I would try to absorb every word he said. There was one occasion that he gave a speech on the benefits of investing in a second form of retirement—a 457 deferred compensation plan. He said it was a very smart investment for the long term. Of course, I did it. It was little things like that that made Chief Tyrell so special. He had tons of book knowledge. And had the biggest impact on my career. I am thankful he is still my friend and will always be a mentor to me," Jimmy said.

Jimmy, despite his twelfth year as a firefighter and paramedic, still has to come into the station every day and make sure everything is in order. While some people may think this becomes boring and routine, for Jimmy, it is a critical part of the job and a process he takes seriously.

"I often compare a fire truck to a giant toolbox," said Jimmy. "Every day when I get to work, I put my gear on the truck then begin checking the medical equipment. The firefighter checks every compartment to make sure things are in order. Then the driver performs a mechanical check which makes sure the engine starts, all the lights, horns, and sirens work, and ensures the tire pressure and everything else is operational—basically all the things that make the truck work. One misstep can literally mean the difference between life and death."

Jimmy added that they have an extensive check list that he follows meticulously. "Even though I know it like the back of my hand, and do not need it anymore, I still make sure everything is in order," he said.

"We also keep the EMS equipment in one compartment so we can access it immediately. We have a drug box with all the medications we need for pain, seizures, overdoses, heart attacks, allergic reactions, and strokes. We also have on board intravenous fluids, a laryngoscope—which allows us to see the vocal cords and insert the endotracheal tube—an airway bag, oxygen tanks, and monitors for cardiac rhythm. There is also an automatic defibrillator that actually tells us when to do compressions and when to stop. We are equally qualified as a full-service ambulance and Advance Life Saving [ALS] vehicle and we have the highest level of medical personnel with us at all times," Jimmy explained.

"I think that is one of the reasons that being a firefighter has been the dream job for me. We are always learning something new and helping people who need us the most. While we have seen the worst of human nature, we have also been part of the best. We get to save lives. Help people. Serve our community. And now that I am married and have a young daughter, I have to constantly remind myself that, if she gets a small cut for example, I cannot be numb to her situation or downplay her injury just because I deal with a lot worse at work. I also realize how vulnerable we all are, and how life can change in a nanosecond. I am fortunate to be part of a team that shares my belief that the risks we take are worth it," Jimmy added.

Fourteen

AMERICA'S HOPE

I will prepare and someday my chance will come.
—Abraham Lincoln

WHILE MOST TEENAGE BOYS ARE CHASING AFTER GIRLS, PLAYING sports, or studying for their SATs, Joseph (Joey) Sheats is suiting up for fires. Though only seventeen years old, he has seen his share of emergencies—nearly as many as men and women twice his age. What is remarkable about Joey is that he has been involved as a first responder in one way or another since he was just thirteen. He is among a dedicated group of young men and women that realize life is more meaningful when they focus on others and recognize the value of serving their communities. For some it is a dream since childhood; for others such as Joey, they were born into a family of service. Regardless, their excitement comes from more than just self-serving endeavors. They are the dreamers. The idealists that hope as adults they will be the ones who keep the world safe, give someone a second chance, and literally extinguish the fires that destroy homes, communities, and lives. Their journeys are exemplified by unwavering determination and one overarching mantra, "How do I get involved?"

Joey Sheats is an old man living in a teenager's body. He is wise beyond his years, knows the value of empathy, and lives every day to perform some type of service. "I have many goals in my life," said Joey. "I guess I got the service bug from my dad, David, who always involved us in the work he did as a 911 dispatcher and constable. I guess you could say that protecting the health and wellbeing of others is what I was born to do."

"Many of my friends are not sure where their lives will lead or how to get there. But I knew as a kid what I wanted to accomplish in my life, and I was not afraid of what I needed to do," said Joey.

Joey grew up in Danielsville, Pennsylvania with his father, David, his stepmother, Janet, and his four brothers Chris, Chantz, Isaac, and Michael. Life was good in his small country town. Joey remembers one time of the year in Danielsville that was especially meaningful and exciting for his large family. "I just loved going to the Lehigh Township Night Out," Joey said. "It was when our community would get together, eat all kinds of food, and dance to the live bands that were actually really good. We also got to meet lots of new people and it was cool hearing about the history of our town," said Joey.

Joey had a passion for working on cars, so he decided to take classes at the Bethlehem Vocational Technical School. "My Dad told me as long as my grades were good, I could get a job someday and make some extra money," Joey said. His thirst for knowledge was insatiable. Joey would spend hours in his driveway tinkering with his parents' vehicles and even considered becoming a professional car mechanic. While excelling in his studies and always wanting to go the extra mile, Joey's leadership abilities were recognized when he was named "Skills USA" vice president for Bethlehem Vocational Technical School, a moniker he cherished.

While Joey loved automobile mechanics, he felt restless and isolated. He realized that it was because he was not collaborating with other people and helping them in one way or another.

So, Joey decided to trade in his car engine for a fire engine. Finally, his life would revolve about his deepest passion—service.

Joey admired his father for the example he set for his sons as a first responder and a man who, without any hesitancy, made it his life's mission to be there for the most vulnerable in society. "Dad is a proud, honorable man who demands respect," said Joey. "I never worried about his safety even though he was a first responder because I knew he had all of the training and knowledge to keep him safe," Joey added. "He was always my hero."

As Joey was considering potential career options that would involve service, he thought he might want to purse becoming a law enforcement officer.

"I thought I wanted to become a police officer," Joey said. His father helped him enroll in Camp Cadet when he was still in high school. The program is a one-week course conducted by the Pennsylvania State Police and the local municipality. The camp's goal is to help young people learn what skills and qualities it takes to become a police officer and gives them an opportunity to experience law enforcement activities first-hand. "We did a lot of physical training, learned the laws regarding law enforcement, and they also taught us leadership skills," Joey said.

"It was a lot of hard work, but I took the program very seriously. It was a great opportunity to gain experience from people actually in the police force, and I could see how determined they were to inspire us to be the type of officers that would make the community proud," Joey shared.

Joey thought that if he were to become a police officer, he wanted as much training as possible. He is a young man who reaches for the stars and never wavers from a challenge. He did so well in the Camp Cadet program that in 2018 he won the "Captain's Award" for his leadership skills, and in 2019 was named a Junior Counselor for the program.

"I was honored to receive these awards, and I was determined to take my new responsibility seriously. I oversaw two squads which were comprised of fifty students. I had to make sure everyone was dressed in the right uniform for each task they were doing that day; I also had to make sure they were always at the right place for their assigned training, along with enforcing rules of the camp," said Joey.

Unfortunately, Joey had to put his goal of being a police officer on hold when the camp was closed due to the COVID-19 pandemic. While Joey was disappointed, he knew that safety always came first. He accepted his situation as many Americans had to do during the outbreak. But after talking to his father, Joey decided to turn his attention to another of his many interests—firefighting.

Joey is a young man who always strives for more. He also had a fire in his belly to be effective in the world, which sounds trite, but to Joey it is who he is at his core. That is one of the reasons he spent his free time exploring new career paths rather than getting in trouble. He was more concerned with advancing his knowledge and getting more certificates than what one might expect from a teenage boy. "I continued to work on my certifications that I learned from the camp because I knew in the future, I wanted to fill the shoes of my heroes; I hoped to be as great as they are one day," Joey said.

It was a cold winter afternoon in November 2021 when Joey had a brainstorm. Since the police camp was closed, and there was no chance of it re-opening anytime soon, Joey, who was now fourteen, decided he wanted to become a firefighter. "I decided I wanted to be part of the fire department because those guys do it all. I knew from my research that I could only be a junior firefighter, but you have to start with baby steps," he said.

"When I first approached the local fire station and asked to talk to the chief, the other firefighters looked at me like I was crazy. I think that was because I was so young. They were nice enough but clearly blew me off, and of course nothing happened," Joey said. "I felt discouraged and decided to wait another year before I went back. I hoped by then they would think I was more mature; I was determined not to give up," said Joey.

When Joey turned fifteen years old, he decided to give firefighting another try. This time he was determined and brought in reinforcements. He asked his father to come with him to the station for support. "I asked the chief if I could apply to be a firefighter and told him about all of my certificates at the police camp and how much I wanted to be part of the fire department. I could not believe that he agreed, and to my surprise, he asked my dad if he wanted an application as well," said Joey.

The last thing Joey's father needed was another avocation, but to help his son achieve his goal he acquiesced.

Being a firefighter would soon become a family affair.

Joey left the fire station with his father, sent in his application, and soon was on his way to the Northampton County Fire School. It was at tough course and Joey spent more than one hundred hours learning the myriad of skills to become a volunteer fireman. It was a labor of love for Joey.

"The bunker gear and air packs alone make this job physically challenging. They are very heavy and cumbersome, and then you must deal with hoses and axes. It was a good thing I was in shape from Camp Cadet training. That was the hard part, but I had no trouble with the classroom work; that was the easy part for me," Joey said.

Joey's first day after his training as a junior volunteer fireman was "awesome."

"I learned so much over the years but since I was only a junior fireman, we were basically gofers. We learned all about the trucks and assisted the guys with getting equipment out of them," said Joey. "We also learned about fire policing, but we were not allowed to get to close to dangerous situations because we were minors," he added. Nevertheless, Joey was thrilled to be part of a firefighting team even though his duties were limited.

"My goal is to be the most qualified and skilled fireman out there," said Joey. "I started doing every online certification that I could find that had to do with being a fireman. I completed two hundred hours of online classes that included fire ground support, hazardous materials awareness, blocking procedures at roadway incidents, fire policing, legal aspects of fire service, and many more. I wanted to be accepted as a fireman, and I knew being knowledgeable about the fire service would prove to the guys that I was capable," he added.

While some of Joey's friends were taking their dates to the prom, he was on the scenes of numerous car accidents, as well as grass and structure fires. He would spend up to twenty hours a week at the station, not counting the time going on fire calls. It was a full plate for a high school student but he was taking it all in. "I was hooked," he said.

"This one time there was a three-alarm fire in an apartment building that was fully engulfed in flames, and all we could do is contain the fire and try to put it out," said Joey. "My job that day was to stand by the back door and feed the hoses to the firemen maintaining a water supply for them." It was an exciting day for the junior fireman who was now part of an adult and elite firefighting team.

Joey was on the scene with his fire company of another incident that affected him deeply. "There was another day when we got a call for a vehicle accident involving a motorcycle. A truck was coming down the road behind a vehicle, and a motorcycle was heading towards them. The truck veered off the road and tried to correct the turn too quickly and lost control," said Joey. The motorcyclist tried to lay down his bike to avoid the truck. Instead of him avoiding the truck, the truck hit the bike and launched over it. "It was terrible and tragic, and the man's head was inside the frame of the truck, and he died on the scene. I was trained to not let calls like this affect me, and it really did not at that moment, but later it did. But I continued doing my job by helping the firemen as I am trained to do," Joey added.

Many of Joey's friends at high school would ask him about what he does at the fire department. "My friends were so curious, and the more stories I told them, the more excited they became. Hey, what young guy would not like hearing how I put out a fire in a burning building or help save someone in a car accident?" Joey recalled. His dramatic stories were so compelling that over time, a few of his friends asked how they could sign up. He was flattered, and it made him feel like a leader—a skill he was proud to learn in the police camp and now as a junior firefighter. "I was psyched. Before I knew it some of my friends were volunteering with me at the fire station," Joey said. "It was awesome!"

Joey taught his friends about the firefighting apparatus and what they needed to know, such as where items belonged in order to assist the firemen as quickly as possible. They also had to learn the jobs around the station that they were required to complete. "When you are a junior firefighter, you do most of the grunt work. We must keep the trucks clean, the garage floor swept, and my favorite, the gross job of cleaning bathrooms," said Joey.

"I tend to go further than most other juniors since they are newer and not familiar with the equipment. For example, I do full function tests of SBA—which is the self-contained breathing apparatus. These are the air packs that are carried on our backs. I make sure they are fully charged, clean, and I document everything. It is very important for all first responders to maintain their equipment, or it could cost them their lives," Joey said.

Joey said that, over time, most of the firefighters loved having the teenagers at the station. Some even took them under their wings and became mentors. "Everything I heard about firefighters being one big family is true," said Joey. "The senior firefighters would take time to teach us all of the tricks of the trade and treated us like we were part of their team for decades," Joey explained.

Aside from spending time each week volunteering at the fire station, Joey still likes to do things those normal teenagers do—playing basketball, baseball, and football and being active in student government. He has even had time to spend with his girlfriend, Crystal, who is proud of Joey's dedication to service.

Joey has done so much in his young life that is inspirational. As he and Crystal were spending one Saturday afternoon together, he talked to her about what his future might hold. Now seventeen, and having experience in law enforcement and firefighting, he wondered if he should be a professional fireman, police officer, auto technician, or maybe enlist in the military.

"I started to develop a plan for my future but had so many choices that I was not sure which direction would be right for me," Joey said.

Then came his epiphany. "I realized that by being in the military and using all of the skills I learned as a junior firefighter, as well as attending the police camp, I could make an even bigger impact," he said.

After serious consideration, as well as discussing his career plans with his father and Crystal, Joey came to a decision. He was going to become a US

Marine. "To me, the Marines are the best of the best when it comes to the military branches. I want to stand proud wearing that uniform," Joey said. Joey thought a tank mechanic job would be something he would explore, but the Marines no longer utilize tanks. *What else would be a good career choice for me in the Marines?* Joey wondered.

Joey drove to the local US Marine recruiter's office where he met Sergeant George. He asked him about his options in the Marines following his high school graduation in 2022 that might involve his skills as a firefighter. "Sergeant George told me that they had a firefighter job in the Marines, and I was pumped! After I filled out all of the paperwork and officially pre-enlisted, a staff sergeant told me I would be filling the only opening left for firefighting. He said I would be stationed at an air base where I would receive Air Rescue Fire Service training (ARFS). I was all in and could not believe that I could continue my love of firefighting and take another oath to serve and protect our country. It was a dream come true for me and it all started with that first day at the fire station," Joey explained.

"He is very brave and respectable. I am proud that he stepped up to serve, not just his community but his country too. I am extremely happy that he is accomplishing his childhood dreams. I know that he will do good, and he will make the folks at home proud. Joey is a kindhearted person, and it is nice to see his hard work paying off. I am here supporting him one hundred percent. Seeing him happy and doing the things he loves is amazing. I am blessed to have him in my life," said Crystal.

Joey, though still a teenager, has some advice for his peers about the importance of service. "Life is all about helping others, not just thinking about yourself. It is not important to have the biggest house, the most expensive clothes, or the top job in your office. It is about caring for others and doing something in life that will improve conditions for those around you. That is what I believe, and I hope to inspire other young people to consider careers in some form of service," Joey explained.

Joey is not sure where the Marines will ultimately send him after Marine boot camp, but wherever he gets stationed, he will be putting out fires and fanning the flames of service.

Fifteen

THE TERROR OF FIRE

I can hear you. The rest of the world hears you. And the people who knocked these buildings down will hear all of us soon.

—President George W. Bush

HEN YOU HAVE LIVED IN THE SAME ZIP CODE FOR MOST OF YOUR life, you have a connection with the people in your neighborhood like no other. Brooklyn, New York, 11234: that is the zip code where Dan Prince grew up. Where he would play T-ball in the back yard with his two brothers. Then when the streetlights would come on, they would race home for supper. No one locked their doors in 11234; the Prince family did not even own any keys. There was not a day that went by where people would not see the Prince brothers shoveling snow from a neighbor's driveway, picking up groceries for a neighbor who was house-bound, or repairing a leak in an elderly neighbor's kitchen. This idyllic life, across the Hudson River from the bustling Borough of Manhattan, was where Dan went to school, worked in a butcher shop, enlisted in the US Navy, and then joined the New York City Fire Department. Fifty-three years later, Dan's sense of solace and serenity were shaken to their core. For on that crisp, sunny fall morning in September, he would be searching for human remains from the rubble that was once New York City's majestic World Trade Center.

"Brooklyn was a beautiful place to grow up," said Dan. "Of the three boys in my family, I was the youngest. We lived in a wonderful area of

Brooklyn. My mom was a homemaker and my dad worked for the New York Transit Authority. Looking back, it was a great neighborhood because we all knew each other and being a good neighbor meant something. When we came home from school, we would check on our neighbors and ask if they needed anything from the store. When we had snowstorms, we took our shovels and removed snow from all our elderly neighbors' steps. We just did it," Dan recalled.

"Dad was very handy and could repair anything. Unfortunately, I was not at all mechanically inclined; I sure wish I were. Dad could take an old washer apart and repurpose the pump so it could be used in a well. There was no appliance that he could not tackle," Dan recalled.

The Prince family lived on 2069 Colemans Street in the Marine Park section of Brooklyn. It was home to the best pizza, bagels, and bialys in the country, according to Dan. For vacations, the Prince clan traveled to the Woodloch Pines Resort in the Pocono Mountains in Pennsylvania—currently voted the "number one family resort" by *USA Today*. Dan and his family loved it so much that years later he purchased a home there. "Woodloch felt a lot like our neighborhood in Brooklyn. It was very family-oriented, everyone hung a flag outside their door, and neighbors were supportive of the military," Dan explained.

Dan was a student at St. Thomas Aquinas and then St. John's Prep before enrolling in Madison High School. While he excelled in math and science and graduated in 1966, he did not have a clear career path, except that he knew he needed to make money.

Since his brother, Jimmy, who was sixteen years older than Dan, was working in a butcher shop on Coney Island, Dan asked if he could work there as well. It was called Major's Butcher Shop and it was a Coney Island legend. "Jimmy got me the job, and I actually started working there as a young teen but all I did was ride my bike—the kind with the big basket on the handlebars—and did the deliveries," Dan recalled. "In the beginning I was doing little odds and ends, and soon learned how to cut up chickens, and all the different meats and how to cut them, too," Dan explained. "Eventually, I worked in the refrigerator and that was cool—literally. I had to take the beef and break it down then make the different cuts. It was a great trade to learn and came in handy when I had a family and worked in the firehouse. The guys would come back from a hunting trip with their deer, and I would skin it for them and cut up the meat. I guess you could say I was a popular guy," said Dan.

Dan was a professional butcher working at Major's for a total of ten years, both full and part time. But at twenty-one years old, he had grander dreams and was longing to get out of Brooklyn and experience the world. So, in 1967 he decided to enlist in the US Navy. After meeting with the recruiter, Dan was stationed at Brooklyn Naval Air Station; he loved it. "I was supposed to be there for just one year, but for one reason or another I wound up spending three years right in Brooklyn. It was disappointing because I had dreams of seeing the world and all I saw was my hometown. It worked out well though because I met nice people and wound-up being assigned to the Police Shore Patrol. That is when I had the idea to become a New York City police officer," Dan said.

Dan left the Navy and headed to City Hall to take the civil service test, which at the time was required to become a bus driver, police officer, or firefighter, for example. "I took the test thinking that I wanted to be a cop, but the first call I got back was from the FDNY. They wanted to hire me. I was so excited that I told the person on the phone, even before they explained the job fully, 'I'll take it!' It turned out to be the best decision I ever made," Dan said.

At just twenty-four years old, Dan became a member of Ladder 156 in the Midwood section of Brooklyn. "It was amazing. I had such a great job and loved going to work because you are always helping people," Dan said. "I loved it so much that even when I was not at work I could not wait to get back and the same goes for vacation. When my vacation dates were set, I was actually disappointed, and I could not wait to get back to work," Dan recalled.

Dan loved riding on the big red truck as it rolled through the streets of Brooklyn. "It was the time of my life," Dan said.

To be a New York City firefighter, you have to complete twelve weeks of official training and then as a "probie" continue that training in the firehouse. "The older guys loved us," Dan said. "You do all the grunt work, and the jokes are really good. When I look back, I realize that this was the greatest experience of my life," he added.

Aside from doing whatever was required in the firehouse, Dan was assigned a position on the truck company, and would accompany an experienced member of the team when there was a call. He would practice a forcible entry or carrying the fire extinguisher with an officer present. "They would always check to see how you are doing and if you are all right," Dan said. "But let me tell you that crawling in total darkness is nothing like you see on television. In fact, I remember my first house fire when we had to go in to complete darkness and I found myself bumping into things. If anyone tells you they are not scared—baloney!" Dan recalled.

Dan said that during the afternoon of his first day at the firehouse, the night crew received a call about a fire not far from the station. There was also a DOA (dead on arrival) as a result. "After the guys returned from the fire call, I could see they were terribly upset because they lost someone. As firefighters, we always blame ourselves, thinking that if we got the call sooner it would have been a much better ending and the victim might have survived," Dan said. "Though I was not part of this fire, I realized I felt the same way. But after everyone talked about their feelings, it was time to get back to work."

When the crew returned, and being the new kid on the block, Dan was assigned the unglamorous job of cleaning the canvas, porous body bag after the corpse was transported to the morgue. (Today, body bags are comprised of plastic with full length zippers that are normally disposed of immediately after the body is removed. There are even newer designs to mitigate toxic exposures due to COVID-19.)

"One of the officers told me, as a probie, that I was the one who had to clean out the body bag; I was numb, but I did what he asked me to do. I also learned that it would be my job to not only clean out the body bags but do all the grunt work that is part of being new," Dan said. "There was lot of skin stuck to the bag and lots of fluids, and it was disgusting. I had to get the cleaning solution, measure so many cups to a gallon, then take a scrub brush and clean it the best I could, then hose the contents down the drain. I will never forget watching all that skin and fluid. But the weird thing was that in one way it was a revelation! Because as a butcher I was accustomed to handling skin, meat, and blood, but even that experience could not have prepared me for this terrible task," Dan added.

Dan said that even as he progressed in his firefighting career, he realized that every fire is different. During the gas crisis in the 1970s, when a ransomware attack forced the Colonial Pipeline to shut down, people were in a panic. They hoarded gasoline and lined up for hours to fill their tanks. "The gas crisis is a perfect example of how there is nothing routine about fires, especially car fires during that time," Dan recalled. "Because people were storing gas in their trucks and cars, they never realized that a gas can explodes. So, we had a slew of car fires during that period. And, because of gas rationing, people were also storing gas in their garages and along the steps going down to their basements."

"There was one house fire like this where there was a sudden explosion. Thank God I was alright but the couple who lived in the house were severely burned. I always tell folks to stop and think about having so much flammable stuff stored in their homes such as gas, propane tanks, paints, and turpentine. And I have seen kerosene heaters, even though they are illegal, still being stored in places that could ignite a fire," Dan explained.

Dan said that he has, unfortunately, had to fight too many fires to count. While all of them are memorable, there are some that to this day still haunt him. It is surprising that Dan still remembers them since there were times he participated in twenty to thirty runs on one fifteen-hour night tour alone. "I remember one Memorial Day when I was at the station helping to get ready for our barbeque in the back courtyard when we got a call to go to a house fire. It was gut-wrenching because that morning the fire took the lives of a couple of kids. Any injuries or deaths of children are the toughest to take," Dan said.

Then just two hours later, Dan and his squad were called back to another fire. As they pulled up to the building, Dan noticed that the windows had iron gates in front of them, mainly for security. "I saw someone outside trying to pull the gate off the window so we knew someone had to be in there. We wound up sawing through the gates, then grabbed the woman who was passed out and pulled her out of the window. It was nuts. We just lost two kids in the morning and now pulled this woman out of a burning building two hours later. By the end of the day, I had hurt my back and shoulder but that is part of the job. That night as I was lying in bed, I felt terrible about losing those kids but at least we saved a woman's life. It was a good feeling in one way, but it did not erase the losses; it just made me feel a little bit better," Dan explained.

Dan said that being a professional firefighter made him highly safety conscious and overly cautious. "It was almost to the point that I was driving people crazy," Dan said. "I was always making sure there was nothing on the stove when the kids or my wife were cooking, and they were not wearing loose clothing either. I was driving them nuts. I was worrying about them all the time and telling them to make sure the appliances and lights were all turned off, and to limit the extension cords we had around the house. One day when I left for work, we had severe storms with a chance of a hurricane developing. I was so worried about my family at home that I imagined trees crashing into the house and all the electrical wires coming down," Dan said. Dan's wife, Debra, was also worried sick when she would hear something on the news about a fireman injured in a fire. "She was a nervous wreck. And at that time, we did not have cell phones so she would call the firehouse to make sure I was okay," Dan added.

One of the most tragic fires Dan recalls was the Waldbaum's fire in the Sheepshead Bay neighborhood of Brooklyn, New York on August 2, 1978. At the time, it was the worst accident involving Brooklyn firefighters in more than ten years. The alarm was sounded at 8:39 a.m., and four fire companies were dispatched as well as a battalion chief. Within minutes thick black smoke was billowing from the building. Firefighters from Ladder Companies 153 and 156 scrambled to the roof, while Engine 254 started to lay down the hoses.

While the firefighters were venting the roof, suddenly the roof caved in and six firefighters were seen running along the ledge. To the first responders on the scene, the firefighters looked like they were ready to jump but instead, fell into the center of the fire. "We lost six fireman and three of them were our guys," Dan said. "They were trying to rescue people inside when suddenly there was a huge blast and the entire roof collapsed. In addition to the three guys from my firehouse who died, there were two others from my battalion who lost their lives that day. And what was so sad was that one of our guys, Billy O'Conner, who I just talked to at the station, told me he got the run and said he would call me later," said Dan. In the meantime, Billy's wife, Louise, came to the firehouse with their kids to pick up Billy to go to the beach, but when he got the call he grabbed his gear, ran to the truck, and was on his way. Louise and the kids followed him in her car and rushed to the site of the fire. "As Billy was climbing the ladder to get to the roof, he turned, noticed his wife and kids watching him from the parking lot, and waved. When Billy finally made it to the roof it suddenly collapsed and he fell into the inferno with the other five firefighters who also perished that day," Dan recalled.

After the roof collapse, firefighters breached the wall and ran in to search for their brothers. "It was heartbreaking," Dan said, as body after body was removed from the store, including Billy's. Each was gently covered with a white sheet or blanket, put on stretchers, and placed in the ambulance.

Before they left the scene, the fallen firefighters were given emergency last rites by FDNY Fire Chaplain Alfred Thompson. Firefighters on the scene wrapped their arms around Billy's wife and children. That would be the last time they would see him alive.

Dan said it took quite a while to get the bodies out of the building and three hours to extinguish the fire. "I did not know about the fire right away because I was at John Jay College taking a summer course. When I got back and came into the firehouse, I saw all the people in the staff cars and the chief in his car. 'What happened?' I asked the chief. 'Where are the victims? How many went to the hospital?' I asked. Then the chief broke the news, no firefighter ever wants to hear. 'We lost them, Dan.'"

Dan said that these words were foreign to him. *No firefighters ever die*, he thought. "I could not grasp the fact the firefighters did die. It was surreal, but the truth is that what we do is among the most dangerous of professions. I cannot even put a timeline on what we did at the time, because it was so traumatic. We had to help the families plan the funerals and made sure to do whatever it took to help. The worst part was that there were eighteen kids involved. Eighteen kids who just lost their dads," Dan said.

Dan and his fellow firefighters lined up to help the families of the fallen who lived in Long Island, Brooklyn, and Staten Island and planned to take care of them. "We did whatever we had to do—from taking them to grocery stores and doctor's appointments to babysitting. There were six funerals, six wakes, and during each one we would stand honor guard at their coffins to show respect and admiration for the sacrifices they made in the line of duty," Dan recalled.

Dan said that the Waldbaum's fire was extremely traumatic and upsetting for him and his entire station. They knew that this was a reality, and tragedy happens, but it does not happen to them. "It was so traumatic going back to work," Dan said. "And the tough part was that it created fear in us for going back up on a roof again. The Waldbaum's fire was always on our minds. But we had to be careful not to relate all roof fires to the supermarket situation. Because they are all different. If you anticipate a roof is spongy, and maybe second guess your instincts, that is not good, and it is when you could get seriously hurt," Dan explained.

Dan said that he is still in touch with the families of the six firefighters who died that day. "We are frequently in touch with the families," Dan said. "We take the kids to ball games, fishing trips, and camping, and now even bring their grandkids. We are always invited to their weddings, communions, and baptisms, and engage in each other's lives. Every year we hold a service in their honor, and we just had our forty-third anniversary memorial mass," Dan added.

Unlike the Walbaum's fire that will always leave a hole in Dan's heart, another near devastating event that targeted the World Trade Center motivated Dan to get involved in a non-profit organization that he still supports today.

The first bombing of the World Trade Center took place in 1993, and while it did not cause the devastation of 9/11, it instilled fear in New Yorkers and people across the country.

A group of Islamic terrorists drove a rented van into the underground parking lot and a 1,200-pound bomb was detonated. It injured more than one thousand people and killed six. Thirty-one firefighters and three police officers were injured. That experience motivated Dan to get more involved with the Firefighter Burn Center Foundation established by firefighters in 1975 to advance burn care research, education, prevention, and treatments. The non-profit organization is located at the New York Hospital-Cornell Medical Center. According to the foundation, its mission is "to make quality burn care available to all who are seriously burned, regardless of age, race, creed, or economic status."

"We would hold fundraisers for firefighters and others who were being treated at the Burn Center," said Dan. "We sold cookbooks, t-shirts, and other items to raise money for the skin bank and burn research and we would also give out fire prevention materials and smoke alarms. We even held an event in the lobby of the Trade Center before the 1993 bombing, and the funny thing was that we spent more time unloading than actually selling what we brought."

But no other burning building in Dan's firefighting career could compare to the terrorist attacks on the World Trade Center on September 11, 2001.

Dan's brother, Ernie, was in the US Army during Vietnam and was suffering from the devastating effects of Agent Orange. His sister-in-law, Kathy, called Dan and asked him if he would travel to Minnesota at the end of August to visit a nursing home and convince her that it was a good place for her husband to reside. Dan had to change the August date they had arranged and instead made it for September 10.

He left that morning on a red eye flight and when the plane landed headed right over to the nursing home. "I was surprised how great it was, and I gave them my blessings and told them I would visit quite often," Dan said. "I went back to the house and was exhausted, so I decided to relax and then go back to work on the twelfth, which was my birthday. That night I went to bed and had a great night's sleep. The next morning, which was September 11, my plan was to pack up and head home," Dan recalled.

After Dan woke up and had his first cup of coffee, he was watching television and saw the first plane hit the North Tower of the World Trade Center. "I knew this was not good right away and that we had been attacked. My wife was going to the doctor that morning in that area and my daughter was in college at NYU. I could not get it touch with anyone. I remember feeling like Forrest Gump and all I wanted to do was run," Dan remembered.

Dan needed to get back home and return to his fire station, but all flights that day were cancelled. Finally, after numerous fits and starts, on Thursday, September 13, Dan finally booked a flight and was on his way back to New York City.

The trip home was horrendous. Dan could not stop thinking about the unimaginable devastation to his beloved New York City, and if his firefighter brothers were involved and okay.

When the plane landed, the remains of the Twin Towers were still smoldering. Dan rushed to the station, grabbed all of his gear, and went to Ground Zero to get to work. Along with his squad and thousands of other firefighters from across the county, each was assigned areas to work, listening for sounds and trying to look for a void where someone could still be alive. "We were digging in the rubble and created bucket brigades. This is where we would pass the buckets back and forth in an attempt to clear the site before any heavy equipment arrived. It was amazing to me that two, 110-story buildings filled with furniture, phones, and filing cabinets, all that remained was dust, rock, and steel. Everything was pulverized and vaporized," Dan said.

"We were at Ground Zero for almost three months, and I would go back and forth because I was assigned to the safety unit. We would pick up fire department gear, find tools, flashlights, and radios and then mark the space where we found them. That way we could say, 'Okay, Engine so and so was working here and the men were from here.' Tragically, mostly all we found were body parts. On the rare occasion that we did bring someone out intact, everyone would stop. We then would create a procession to show respect for all of the fallen victims," Dan said.

"It was so hard walking on broken-up debris and feeling the heat of the smoke coming from the fires, underground. I knew one hundred of the 343 firefighters who died that day, and it was another heartbreak," Dan recalled. Since 9/11, the number of firefighter deaths has increased primarily from the effects of inhaling toxic materials.

In a 2021 report by the Fire Department of New York, it was revealed that approximately 410,000 first responders and others who spent weeks working after 9/11 inhaled toxic materials. Twenty years later, another 268 firefighters have died from 9/11–related diseases and the numbers are still rising. Other chronic illnesses include gastroesophageal reflux (GERD), cancer, blood disorders, skin cancer, and chronic symptoms such as cough or shortness of breath, which could be a sign of asbestos exposure.[1]

"I am sure that at some point that number will increase among police officers, construction workers, and other first responders, not just firefighters who were working at Ground Zero that day. I have some respiratory issues as a result of my participation and also GERD," Dan said. "I think we ingested dust and other toxic particles when we ate fast food for all of those months. People would be walking around feeding us hamburgers, and we were so hungry that we ate everything including drinking all those cups of coffee. The particles were probably even in the water cups. But people were just trying to help," Dan recalled.

In the weeks and months after 9/11, Dan and his firefighter brothers and sisters stayed in contact for moral support but also to help the families of the fallen deal with the loss of their husbands, fathers, and children. "We would do things such as fixing problems in their houses or cars or just being there to comfort the families," Dan said. "We would also attend as many funerals as we could. It was tough because some days there were a dozen funerals. But the bagpipers made sure that they had bagpipers on scene for every funeral. It was a tough job because they only had about seventy pipers available at all times to help."

"I was going to the station and working all day, then getting off and running to funerals, then going home and back to work. That was tough. And it was beginning to wear on us because we rarely found people alive. I hoped that we would the next day, and the day after, but tomorrow never came; it was heartbreaking," said Dan.

Dan said there was tremendous support for firefighters, first responders, and construction workers in the aftermath of 9/11. "We had counseling, clergy visits, and a great outpouring from people who wanted to help.

---

1   "After 9/11 Toxins," Fire Department of New York, 2021, https://www.nyc.gov.

We even had massage and acupuncture therapists; the love was amazing. When I look at where we are now in the country it depresses me. We had such love back then. I remember all the buses and vans leaving the area and citizens lining up on the streets cheering us on. It was overwhelming and helped me a lot," Dan recalled.

But there was another tragic moment that Dan recalls in the aftermath of 9/11. "One fellow firefighter I worked with, Bobby Crawford, was found on Thanksgiving Day. We had to go to his house to inform his wife and family, which was heartbreaking. The family thought we came by just to say 'hello' but we were there to inform them that Bobby's body was finally found. That was an emotional day, but his wife said she was relieved that at least he was recovered," said Dan.

"September 11 was a really tough day, but I am thankful because if I did not visit my brother, I might have been one of the statistics. Being at Ground Zero for three months and helping my fallen brothers and their families during what was among the worst times of my life and the country's was a blessing," Dan said.

Months after 9/11, Dan continued his work on the investigation team. He and his colleagues frequently suffered from "survivor's guilt," but he realized they did the best they could. Before the recovery efforts were officially shut down at Ground Zero, and the site was prepared for cleanup, issues arose among a group of first responders. "Some of the guys could not accept their brothers were lost and would not leave the site and that did create a problem for a while," Dan said. "There were even a few first responders who were arrested, and as a result, the decision was made to wait a bit longer before any demolition took place."

Seven years after 9/11, Dan, now sixty years old, decided it was time to retire. But he quickly changed his mind when the next big conflagration occurred; he could not stand by and run away from danger.

The fire took place on August 18, 2007, at Deutsche Bank, right across the street from the World Trade Center site. The fire was ignited by a worker's cigarette. It turned the building into a blazing inferno with thick black smoke and flames roaring throughout the building. The blaze killed two firefighters and injured more than one hundred.

As part of the demolition work a standpipe—the main source of water—was cut and with no water available the fire raged out of control. "This should not have happened!" Dan exclaimed. "I was in the safety battalion and doing the investigation and I said, 'I cannot take it anymore.' I really wanted to stay but my emotions went back down there again and triggered PTSD. I imagined being trapped in the burning building and running out of air. It gave me nightmares and that is when I knew I had to go," Dan added.

After a grand farewell party, Dan decided to officially volunteer with the Fire Family Transport, a non-profit organization that he got to know after the 1993 World Trade Center bombing as well as when he was volunteering with the Burn Center. It was then that Jimmy Curran, president of the Firefighters Burn Center Foundation, and Pat Concannon, founder of the Fire Family Transport Foundation, had a meeting and decided to buy a van to transport family members and firefighters to the Burn Center and local hospitals. Many of his retired firefighter brothers were already involved, and Dan wanted to do something in retirement that his heart told him was right.

"I wanted to continue taking care of the firefighter families and firefighters who had injuries or illnesses. It was a great way to still be involved with the fire department, and it was good therapy," said Dan.

Dan has been volunteering with the Fire Family Transport for the past thirteen years. He helped to raise money for vans that would transport patients and families to doctor's appointments, hospital visits, and funerals.

During one of the many fundraisers Dan was involved with, he met Gary Sinise, the actor, philanthropist, and founder of the Gary Sinise Foundation that supports military members and their families, veterans, and first responders. "Gary hosted a concert with his Lt. Dan Band and the money raised helped finish the *Wall of Remembrance* in Coney Island, New York, which had the names and photos of all the 417 first responders who died on 9/11 etched on the wall. Gary also generously donated three more vans over the years [to Fire Family Transport]," Dan said. "In addition, the families of the fallen firefighters got involved as well and were kind enough to donate even more vans. All the money we raised went to providing fuel for the vans, insurance, maintenance, and EZ-Passes; no one was ever paid, we are just enthusiastic volunteers," Dan added.

Gary's dedication inspired Dan to not just support his fellow firefighters, but to also help wounded warriors. He began visiting them at Walter Reed National Military Medical Center in Bethesda, Maryland two times every month, as well as attending Christmas and Super Bowl parties. That involvement with the foundation's philanthropic efforts led Gary to name Dan as one of the Gary Sinise Foundation ambassadors, a role he relishes. (Ambassadors are selected based upon their patriotism and character.) Dan and his fellow ambassadors represent the foundation through public appearances, speaking engagements and leadership opportunities.

"I tell people I feel like I won the lottery ticket," Dan explained. "Doing what I do now, this is my lottery ticket. Giving back is thanking God for everything you have been given and realizing how blessed you are. It is a rewarding feeling to see that smile on someone's face, or a tear dry up and go away; that says it all. I have the passion and drive and am not a taker; this is now my life's work," Dan said.

Dan has been paying it forward all of his life. And volunteerism has always been a family affair. For years Dan has brought his daughter, Heather, and her daughter, Gracie, with him to the Burn Center on numerous occasions. When Heather was a child, she played the role of an elf at a Christmas show there and an Easter bunny as well. The family would also bring toys they collected for children who were patients at the Sloan Cancer Center. Every year Heather and Gracie would also visit Walter Reed and give the wounded warriors and their families Girl Scout cookies. There would be no end to the Prince family's dedication to service.

"This is my idea of a great retirement—being with my family and supporting my brothers and sisters who are my heroes," Dan said. "I would not trade my life now for anything in the world."

Sixteen

CALLED TO ACT

Never doubt that a small group of thoughtful, committed citizens can change the world;
indeed, it's the only thing that ever has.
—Margaret Mead, cultural anthropologist and author

FIRST RESPONDERS RISK IT ALL TO SERVE AND PROTECT THEIR FELLOW Americans. Then there are others who, because of their belief that service matters, seek to effect positive outcomes in less dramatic but meaningful pursuits. Such is the case with a US Marine veteran and advocate for social change, Samuel P. Royer, who is also a co-author of this book. Though not a first responder, Sam had the advantage of growing up with his sister, Amy Royer, a passionate EMT, who is also profiled in the book. We were compelled to add Sam's story to *Called to Serve* because we believe his efforts to support police, fire, and emergency medical professionals are inspirational. This is his story.

Sam is a businessman with one singular goal—to give first responders the means to achieve the American dream of affordable home ownership. He knows that serving his country is among the most noble of pursuits and the most rewarding of the human experience. As a veteran, Sam and his band of brothers and sisters have taken advantage of the Veterans Administration benefits, which are a way of recognizing them for their service and sacrifice.

However, as Sam became friends with first responders, including police officers, firefighters, emergency medical professionals, and teachers, he

167

realized that, unlike military members, they do not have the ability to purchase a home without logistical restrictions and exorbitant fees. For them, the dream of homeownership may never become a reality. Rather than sit back and accept the discrepancy, Sam decided he had to do something to make that right. Though not a professional K-Street lobbyist, but rather national director of Heroes First Home Loans and a twenty-five-year mortgage professional, he was on a mission. His goal: to give first responders and educators a loan program that would ease the path to owning a home with the same benefits already available to military members and veterans.

"It was almost two years ago when a police officer friend of mine told me that she could not afford a down payment for a home she was interested in buying as well as the mortgage insurance. This is a woman who every day risks her life and deals with so much just to keep us safe and she cannot afford a home? It was unacceptable to me, and I realized I had to do something to make that right," Sam said.

Sam's strategy was to find a way to change how first responders and teachers pay for their homes and make the process affordable just as it is for military members, veterans, and their families. In the process of conducting research and involving his team as well as his friend from high school, George McElwee, who worked for former Congressman Charlie Dent (R-PA) and now owns a consulting firm, Sam discovered his dream was within reach.

Together, they came up with a novel idea—to approach the US Congress with a concept for a bill that would solve the problem and provide first responders a path toward affordable home ownership. "We came up with 'The HELPER Act' which stands for 'Homes for Every Local Protector, Educator, and Responder.' The goal of the proposed bill would be to provide federally-funded affordable mortgage solutions to our police, firefighters, EMS workers, and teachers," Sam explained.

Sam and George put together the concept of "The HELPER Act" and the next step was to arrange a meeting with Florida Congressman John Rutherford to get his feedback. Sam's primary goal was for Congressman Rutherford to endorse the idea and become one of the bill's sponsors. "I was thrilled that Congressman John Rutherford, who was also the former sheriff of Jacksonville, Florida, was excited about the idea, as were his staff. They helped us draft 'The HELPER Act' legislation, and within ten months we had a solid piece of proposed legislation that we could use to find co-sponsors and ultimately get the bill passed into law," said Sam.

In May 2021, "The HELPER Act" was introduced on the floor of the US House of Representatives by a group of bipartisan House Members including Al Lawson (D-FL); John Katko (R-NY); and Bonnie Watson Coleman (D-NJ). The bill currently has the support of seventeen Democrats and eleven Republicans and that number is still growing.

"Teachers, paramedics, EMTs, law enforcement officers, and firefighters are the cornerstone of our American communities. It is time to help make the dream of home ownership a reality for these local heroes, and 'The HELPER Act' would do just that. It builds on the success of the VA home loan program to offer a similar benefit to first responders and educators across the country. 'The HELPER Act' would bolster recruitment and retention for critical professions and says 'thank you' to those who serve our communities every day," said Congressman Rutherford.

Sam did have to assure members of Congress and help them understand that the bill would not cost the Federal Government additional funds. "We purposely added to the legislation how the program would be funded," explained Sam. It would be administered under Housing and Urban Development (HUD) or the Federal Housing Administration (FHA) and allow any qualifying first responder to go to any FHA-approved lender for 100 percent financing, no down payment, no monthly mortgage insurance, and an upfront mortgage insurance premium around 3.6 percent. This would save the first responder around $90 a month based on a home purchase of $200,000 and would enhance their buying power, according to Sam.

Sam said that the federal government, though responsible for the loan default, should be confident that first responders are among the most responsible potential home buyers. "Seriously, I can tell you that police, firefighters, teachers, and EMS workers are the least likely to not pay their loans. They are among the most responsible and honorable people I know, and I would highly doubt they would be the ones to default on their mortgage payments," Sam added.

With Congressman Rutherford on board, Sam and his team began to lobby other members of Congress and their staffs to become co-sponsors of 'The HELPER Act' and support the nation's first responders, who Sam believes are America's unsung heroes.

The next step in Sam's plan was to get the bill introduced in the US Senate. Having 'The HELPER Act' moving through both the House and Senate multiplied its chances of becoming law. On October 18, 2021, Senator Marco Rubio (R-FL), from Sam's home state of Florida, and Senator Jon

Ossoff (D-GA) introduced the companion bill. "I was honored that both senators and their staffs were 100 percent behind the proposed bipartisan legislation," Sam said.

"First responders and teachers work tirelessly to serve our communities, and they have faced incredibly difficult circumstances over the past two years," Rubio said. "As housing prices continue to skyrocket, our bill would help ensure that teachers and first responders can own a home in the communities they dutifully serve."

Another motivation for Sam was his own military service as a US Marine. While he only served for four years, which he deeply regrets, Sam was able to take advantage of the benefits that the Veterans Administration offers. After he left the military, and as his career progressed, he became friends with first responders and was appalled that they had trouble buying a new home because the upfront costs were out of reach.

"Since World War II, the US government has passed legislation to give military members, veterans, and their families support following their military service. I had to do something to help all of the first responders who have risked their lives as well," Sam added.

In 1944, the GI Bill was passed into law, providing benefits to returning military members and their families including tuition assistance to help them assimilate back into the civilian world and compensate them for their sacrifice and service. After September 11, and with a new generation of warfighters returning home, the GI Bill offered enhanced benefits through the Veterans Administration and was signed into law by President George W. Bush in 2008 and took effect in 2009.

Among the enhanced benefits included are tuition and fees reimbursement, a monthly allowance, access to military base services, discounts on good and services, home loan discounts, and much more. Over the years, millions of military members, veterans, and their families took advantage of the GI Bill, graduated from universities, colleges, and trade schools, purchased homes, and received access to military medical centers for the rest of their lives.

"This was not the case for our nation's unsung heroes—first responders who have put themselves in harm's way by climbing into burning buildings, leaving home every day not knowing if they will return alive, resuscitating victims who are in cardiac arrest, preventing a disturbed student from brandishing a weapon in class, and suffering debilitating mental health issues," Sam said. "They risk their lives every day to keep us healthy and

safe, console us during unspeakable tragedies, and have to rely on the generosity of their professional associations, unions, non-profit organizations,
and complete strangers."

Sam's vision, along with the members of Congress who have lent their
support and the advocates he has met along his journey, is to pass 'The
HELPER Act' and have it become the law of the land. "This legislation will
help first responders from across the country achieve the dream of home
ownership. I would feel like I have done my job when I can say that these
heroes can have a roof over their head and live happy and healthy lives. It
is the least I can do to thank them for their service not just in words but by
actions. I am thankful for the support of the members of Congress who
believed in my mission and supported these amazing men and women,"
Sam added.

Sam's relentless advocacy and drive have been an inspiration to everyone he has touched along the way. Who says one person cannot change the
world? Sam may just be one of those committed citizens who has.

—Mike Hardwick and Dava Guerin

EPILOGUE

WE HOPE AS THE YEARS GO BY AND THE TSUNAMI OF DIVISION recedes, Americans will appreciate—and yes, even revere—the service and sacrifice of our first responders. These brave men and women put themselves in harm's way with little regard for their own safety. With every sunrise and sunset, they wear their uniforms with pride; they do not consider themselves heroes. It is that belief that service is their mission that sets them apart from the rest. They run toward danger, not away from it, often risking their own lives to save the lives of complete strangers. Unfortunately, there are not enough stories of first responders' selflessness and professionalism, but hopefully, after reading this book, they will become abundantly evident.

Why would 257,700 paramedics and EMTs, 1,115,000 career and volunteer firefighters, and 800,000 police officers—careers that are inherently dangerous and have the possibility of causing physical and psychological harm and even death—choose these professions?

If you ask any one of the law enforcement professionals, emergency medical professionals, and firefighters profiled in this book, you already know the answer. They were called to serve. Some grew up in drug- and crime-infested neighborhoods where addicts and gangs were the norm. Others came from modest means, where families were torn apart by divorce or illness, or even grew up in a cult where followers were told that the earth was not round but pear-shaped. And some of the men and women in the book grew up in loving and nurturing homes.

But the one common denominator with all of the heroes in *Called to Serve* is that they were surrounded by parents and mentors who believed that service to others was valued and encouraged. As children, they learned the meaning of giving back to others by simple and random acts of kindness.

Shoveling snow that piled up in a neighbor's driveway, picking up a gallon of milk and a dozen eggs for an elderly house-bound couple, or dreaming of extinguishing fires as a young teen.

Why should we care? The answer is simple—because we need them. They make our world safer, healthier, and more secure.

Imagine what life would be like if someone we loved was experiencing a cardiac arrest and there was no one there to stabilize him or her? Or if a loved one fell down the stairs and could not get up from the floor? If a person were trapped inside a burning building and there were no firefighters on hand to rescue them? Or if someone were breaking into our house, holding a gun to our heads, or drinking and driving and there were no police officers racing to the scene to arrest the perpetrator?

There would no doubt be chaos, confusion, and even death. We do not disregard the fact that among America's first responders there are those who have dishonored their profession; we all know who they are and that is not acceptable. As Sheriff Matt Crisafulli said, "There is nothing a good police officer hates more than a bad police officer."

It is our hope that when you have finished reading the sixteen inspiring stories in *Called to Serve*, you will be moved—as we were—to reach out to those in need in your community. You do not have to wear a uniform or a badge to do that. But for those who do, we will forever be grateful. We will have a deeper understanding and appreciation of the service and sacrifice of our first responders and realize that they chose this line of work for all the right reasons.

Finally, we want to thank them for letting us into their lives and sharing their amazing and inspiring personal stories with us and you, the reader.

ABOUT THE AUTHORS

Lawson H. (Mike) Hardwick, III is a seasoned veteran in the mortgage and banking industries and has worn multiple hats throughout his forty-plus-year career. As founder and chief executive officer of Brentwood, a Tennessee-based Churchill Mortgage Corporation, Hardwick oversees a team of over a thousand teammates, all dedicated to serving others and aiding homebuyers in their journey to debt-free homeownership.

Prior to founding Churchill Mortgage, Hardwick gained a wealth of knowledge and expertise through positions as a mortgage, insurance, and real estate broker, and continued to flex his entrepreneurial mind through various ventures. The first half of his career was spent in commercial and investment banking with two nationally known firms. In the early 1980s, he started a condominium conversion company, which grew to be one of the largest in the nation. Shortly after the peak of that business, Hardwick became one of the principal founders of Franklin National Bank in Franklin, Tennessee, where he served as an executive vice president until 1992 when he founded Churchill Mortgage. He continued serving on the Board of Directors for Franklin National Bank for several years thereafter (later acquired by Fifth Third Bank).

One of Hardwick's proudest accomplishments is his autobiography, *Keep Chopping Wood*, which was published in 2016 and gives an insider's glimpse at not only his personal experiences and remarkable journey from humble beginnings, but an in-depth, realistic look into the business world.

Hardwick obtained his bachelor's degree in Theology and Music from Gateway College (now known as Urshan College) and his Bachelor of Business Administration in Finance from Belmont University. Outside of work, Hardwick is a member of the Forbes Finance Council, a founder and board member of Studio Bank, Real Estate Services of America, Escrow

175

Services of Tennessee, Churchill Agency, and Equity Express. He presently serves on the Tennessee Housing & Development Board and has served on many boards and committees, including Friends of the Arts Board at Belmont University, Premier Speakers Bureau, and the Finance & Endowment Committee for Christ Church Nashville. Hardwick is a lifelong resident of Middle Tennessee.

Dava Guerin is the co-author of *The Eagle on my Arm: How the Wilderness and Birds of Prey Saved a Veteran's life* (University Press of Kentucky, 2019); *Laughing at Myself* with Secretary Dan Glickman (University Press of Kansas, 2021); *Rebuilding Sgt. Peck: How I Healed Body and Soul After Afghanistan* (Skyhorse Publishing, April 2019); *Unbreakable Bonds: The Mighty Moms and Wounded Warriors of Walter Reed,* (Skyhorse Publishing, November 2016) and *Vets and Pets: Wounded Warriors and the Animals That Help Them Heal* (Skyhorse Publishing, September 2018). She is also the co-author of two memoirs—*Presidents, Kings and Convicts* with former US Congressman Bob Clement (D-TN); and *Keep Chopping Wood*, with Mike Hardwick, CEO of Churchill Mortgage Corporation.

Guerin is also a communications consultant and writer, and was the former communications director for the US Association of Former Members of Congress in Washington, DC. She was also president of Guerin Public Relations, Inc., a full-service communications firm before becoming an author; profile editor of *Local Living Magazine* and *Bucks Living Magazine*; senior vice president of Weighman Public Relations; and worked in senior level positions for Ketchum Public Relations and the Philadelphia Convention and Visitors Bureau. She also volunteers her time helping wounded warriors, veterans, and their families as well as supporting the Barbara Bush Foundation for Family Literacy and the Gary Sinise Foundation. Guerin has a BA degree in Literature from Goddard College and graduated Summa Cum Laude from Temple University with a MEd degree in Organizational Behavior.

Sam Royer believes in helping American Heroes achieve the American Dream—buying their own home. As national director of Heroes First Home Loans, Royer helps provide affordable mortgage financing for active and retired military members, police, firefighters, healthcare workers, educators, and other civil servants. His experience in the US Marine Corps and ability to forge relationships with frontline workers have allowed Royer to stake out a unique position in the industry while fueling his passion to give back to those who take care of us. He has been a consistent top performer in the mortgage business and has garnered numerous awards for his work, including from the Daytona Beach Police Department, Volusia County Sheriff's Office, and Flagler County Sheriff's Office. A US Marine (Ret.) he is currently the national director of Heroes First Loans Division of Churchill Mortgage Corporation. He is active in raising funds and awareness of Police, Fire, and EMS professionals in Florida as well as advocating on their behalf. He is a dedicated volunteer, helping provide food and other needed services to first responders during local emergencies.